W9-BIA-359

BRIGHAM'S

Technology

SUPPLEMENT

EUGENE F. BRIGHAM
University of Florida

SOUTH-WESTERN

THOMSON LEARNING

Australia · Canada · Mexico · Singapore · Spain · United Kingdom · United States

SOUTH-WESTERN

THOMSON LEARNING

Technology Supplement

Eugene F. Brigham

COPYRIGHT © 1999
by South-Western, a division of
Thomson Learning. Thomson
Learning™ is a trademark used
herein under license.

Printed in the United States of
America
6 7 8 9 07 06 05

For more information

For more information
contact South-Western,
5191 Natorp Boulevard,
Mason, Ohio, 45040.
Or you can visit our Internet site
at: http://www.swcollege.com

ALL RIGHTS RESERVED.
No part of this work covered by
the copyright hereon may be
reproduced or used in any form
or by any means–graphic,
electronic, or mechanical,
including photocopying,
recording, taping, Web
distribution or information
storage and retrieval systems–
without the written permission of
the publisher.

For permission to use material
from this text or product, contact
us by
Tel (800) 730-2214
Fax (800) 730-2215
http://www.thomsonrights.com

ISBN: 0-03-023372-0

PREFACE

This *Technology Supplement* is intended to provide students with the skills necessary to use the technological tools most commonly applied in financial analysis: namely, financial calculators and spreadsheets. Also, since presentation of results is an important part of the managerial process, we provide some information on presentation software. Of course, it is impossible to turn someone into a calculator or spreadsheet or presentation software expert with short tutorials, but an understanding of the tutorials in this supplement will enable students to perform all of the calculator analyses – such as time value of money and linear regression – discussed in the text. furthermore, an understanding of the spreadsheet tutorial will provide students with the skills necessary to create, modify, and use the typical spreadsheet models that accompany cases, and an understanding of presentation software will help students convey their findings and recommendations.

The supplement is divided into three major parts: Part I, which contains several sections dealing with the most commonly used financial calculators; Part II, which contains the spreadsheet tutorial; and Part III, which contains the Powerpoint presentation tutorial. Users of this publisher's finance textbooks are authorized to have sections, or this entire supplement, copied and sold to students (at cost).

Dana Aberwald Clark, Brent Gibbs, Darryll Parker, and Dan Zinn helped create the tutorials, and Carol Stanton and Susan Purcell produced the final manuscript. We have tried to make the *Technology Supplement* as clear and error-free as possible; however, there are almost certainly some mistakes and unclear sections. Any suggestions for improving this supplement would be greatly appreciated.

Eugene F. Brigham
Department of Finance
College of Business Administration
University of Florida
Gainesville, FL 32611-2017

March 1999

CONTENTS OF THE TECHNOLOGY SUPPLEMENT

Introduction to Financial Calculators

The history of the modern pocket calculator dates back to the creation of the abacus. The abacus, which was invented thousands of years ago, offered an easy way of adding and subtracting. Plus, it could also be used for multiplication and division. While this was a revolutionary innovation in its time, the evolution of calculating devices over the following centuries proved to be somewhat slow and methodical. As America moved through the industrial revolution, mechanical calculators became more sophisticated, but they were still very bulky and relatively limited in their computational capabilities. However, as with many other products, the evolution of calculating devices progressed dramatically as the world entered the age of electronics.

Since the invention of the integrated circuit in 1958, the power to incorporate more and more capabilities into a single chip of silicon has truly changed the world. At that time, the modern era of microelectronics was in its infancy. In 1967, engineers were still in the beginning stages of exploring the uses and advantages of metal-oxide semiconductor (MOS) integrated circuits, invented only nine years earlier by Texas Instruments. In 1967, a Texas Instruments team of engineers developed the first electronic handheld calculator. This marked the first time MOS integrated circuits were used in a product that had large commercial market potential.

Creating this miniature machine entailed more than just figuring out the logic and executing it as integrated circuits. The complexity, small size, and low power required by the calculator were unprecedented. Although the device was only capable of performing basic arithmetic functions (addition, subtraction, multiplication, and division), the handheld calculator was truly an amazing accomplishment for its time.

Initially, handheld calculators were very expensive relative to their limited calculating capabilities. Continued advances in computer technology, however, have dramatically improved the price/performance ratio. In fact, advanced calculations that 25 years ago would have required a room full of computing devices can now be quickly and easily performed with a handheld calculator that costs less than $40.00. All of the major calculator manufacturers produce calculators which can be used for basic arithmetic functions as well as for scientific, statistical, or financial calculations.

Financial calculators are designed to meet the special needs of professionals working in a finance function as well as finance students. Early financial calculators were distinguished from "regular" calculators by virtue of having built-in time value of money functions such as present value and future value of lump sums and annuities. Today, financial calculators run the gamut from only basic time value functions to relatively expensive calculators that allow users to program their own financial algorithms.

This tutorial, which focuses specifically on financial calculators, is intended to provide an overview of how to perform the most common types of finance problems. The models covered are the Texas Instruments BAII PLUS, the SHARP EL-733A, and the Hewlett-Packard HP-12C, HP-10B, and HP-17BII. This is by no means an exhaustive list of financial calculators, but these specific models were chosen for three reasons. First, all of the models selected are capable of performing advanced financial calculations including, but not limited to, time-value-of-money, cash flow analyses, and linear regression. Second, these calculators appear to be the most commonly sold and used on college campuses. Finally, all of these calculators can be purchased for under $100, so they are affordable to the average college student. In fact, the EL-733A, HP-10B, and HP-12C typically sell for under $40.00. Obviously, there is some trade-off between price and performance, but any of the calculators outlined in this tutorial are more than adequate for most college-level finance courses.

To begin, look at the face of the calculator. Every key (except two, the gold shift key and the purple shift key) on the 10BII has at least two functions: each key's primary function is noted in white on the key itself, while each key's secondary function is noted in gold above the key. To use the function on the key, simply press the key. To access the gold function at the bottom of each key, first press the key with the solid gold face, which we will call the "gold shift" key, and then press the desired function key. Likewise, to access the purple "STATS" function above some of the keys, first press the key with the solid purple face, which we will call the "purple shift" key, and then press the desired function key. (Note that the gold and purple shift keys are near the lower left corner of the calculator keyboard.)

Turning the Calculator On and Off

To turn on the calculator, press ON .

Note that the ON key is on the lower left corner of the keyboard—the face of the key has a white "ON," while the word "OFF" appears below the key in gold. Also, we will designate keys throughout this tutorial by the use of small boxes, as above. To conserve the battery, the calculator turns itself off about 10 minutes after your last keystroke.

To turn the calculator off, press G OFF .

Here we are using the square labeled "G" to represent the gold shift key. Thus, the keystrokes to turn the calculator off are (1) press the gold shift key, and (2) then press the "ON" key. Thus, by pressing the gold shift key first, we are activating the gold function below the "ON" key, which is the "OFF" function. Also, note that pressing the gold shift key places a little "SHIFT" symbol in the lower left corner of the display. Press the gold shift key again and the symbol goes away. Likewise, pressing the purple shift key places a "STATS" symbol in the lower left area of the display. The $\boxed{G}$ key is a toggle key that switches back and forth between the "regular" and the "gold" functions. Likewise, the $\boxed{P}$ key is a toggle between "regular" and "STATS" functions. The $\boxed{G}$ key and the $\boxed{P}$ key are like typewriter shift keys. After you press $\boxed{G}$, look only at the gold writing, and after you press $\boxed{P}$, look only at the purple writing. In this tutorial, whenever you see $\boxed{G}$ or $\boxed{P}$, the label on the next key is the gold or purple label corresponding to the key, not the label on the key itself.

Note that the calculator has a continuous memory, so turning it off does not affect any data stored in the calculator.

Clearing the Calculator

To clear the calculator's memory, press $\boxed{G}$ $\boxed{\text{CLEAR ALL}}$.

Clearing the calculator is very important, since unwanted data in memory can result in improper calculations, and hence wrong answers. It is best to get into the habit of automatically clearing memory before starting a calculation. Occasionally, you may purposely want to save data, but, in general, you will be entering all new data, so starting with a clear memory is the safest approach.

There are three different levels of clearing data:

$\boxed{G}$ $\boxed{\text{CLEAR ALL}}$ clears all memory and the display.

$\boxed{C}$ clears the entire display, but not the memory.

$\boxed{\leftarrow}$ clears numbers on the display one at a time.

Changing the Display

Enter 5555.5555.

To change the number of decimal places from 2 to 4, press [G] [DISP] [4]. Now, 5,555.5555 is displayed.

To change from 4 decimal places to 2, press [G] [DISP] [2]. Now, 5,555.56 is displayed. (Rounding is automatic.)

We usually set the display to 2 places, which is especially convenient when working with dollars and percentages. However, we often use 4 places when dealing with interest rates and rates of return that are entered as decimals.

If periods and commas are reversed, press [G] [./,] . (Many European countries use a ./, convention that is the opposite of ours.)

Note that "PEND" means something is pending. For example, press [4] [÷] . The calculator is waiting for the denominator, so "PEND" appears in the display.

Enter [6] and [=] to get 0.67.
Press [G] [DISP] [4] to see 0.6667.
Press [G] [DISP] [2] to shift back to 2 decimal places.

To control the brightness of the display, hold down [ON] and press [+] or [-].

Periods per Year (P/YR) Setting

One important setting that can cause problems is the periods per year setting. To check the current setting, press ⬚G⬚ and then press and hold down ⬚CLEAR ALL⬚. The display shows the setting for periods / year. The calculator comes pre-set at 12 periods per year, that is, it assumes calculations will be done on a monthly basis. However, finance textbook problems generally leave the calculator at 1 P/YR.

Press ⬚1⬚ ⬚G⬚ ⬚P/YR⬚.

Now the calculator is set to assume 1 P/YR. To confirm this setting, press and hold ⬚G⬚ ⬚CLEAR ALL⬚. Unless needed for other work, we generally leave the calculator setting at 1 P/YR.

Time Value of Money (TVM)

The TVM keys are located on the top row of the keyboard.

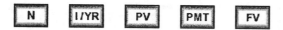

In general, TVM problems involve five variables—four are known and the fifth is unknown.

Lump Sums

To begin, we consider TVM calculations with single (lump) sums. In this situation, we do not use the PMT key, so be sure to either clear all, which sets the payment (PMT) equal to 0, or enter 0 as the PMT when entering the input data. If you know any four variables, you can find the value of the fifth.

Example 1:

What is the FV of $100 after 3 years if the interest rate is 26 percent? First, clear by pressing [G] [CLEAR ALL].

Next, enter the following data:

3 [N]

26 [I/YR]

100 [PV]

0 [PMT]

To determine the FV simply press [FV] and the FV of -$200.04 is displayed.

The HP is programmed so that if the PV is + then the FV is displayed as - and vice versa, because the HP assumes that one is an inflow and the other is an outflow. When entering both PV and FV, one must be entered as negative and the other as positive.

Example 2:

What is the PV of $500 due in 5 years if the interest rate is 10 percent? Clear first and then enter the following data.

5 [N]

10 [I/YR]

0 [PMT]

500 [FV]

Pressing the [PV] key reveals that $310.46 will grow to $500 in 5 years at a 10 percent rate.

Example 3:

Assume a bond can be purchased today for $200. It will return $1,000 after 14 years. The bond pays no interest during its life. What rate of return would you earn if you bought the bond?

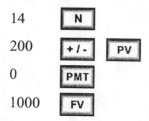

14   N

200   + / -   PV

0   PMT

1000   FV

Simply press the I/YR key and the HP calculates the rate of return to be 12.18 percent.

Remember that the HP is programmed so that if the PV is + then the FV is displayed as - and vice versa because the HP assumes that one is an inflow and other is an outflow. When entering both PV and FV values, one must be negative and one positive.

Now suppose you learn that the bond will actually cost $300. What rate of return will you earn?

Override the -200 by entering 300 + / - PV , then press I/YR to get 8.98 percent. If you pay more for the bond, you earn less on it. The important thing, though, is that you can do "what if" analyses with the calculator.

Now, press G OFF to turn off the calculator. Next, turn on the calculator ON . The display shows 0.00. Is the memory erased? Not completely. What was on the screen is gone, but press RCL N to get N = 14. The other memory registers also retain information unless you press G CLEAR ALL .

Ordinary Annuities

Example 1:

What is the FV of an annuity of $100 paid at the end of each year for 5 years if the interest rate equals 6 percent?

Now, enter the following data:

5 $\boxed{\text{N}}$

6 $\boxed{\text{I/YR}}$

0 $\boxed{\text{PV}}$

100 $\boxed{\text{+/-}}$ $\boxed{\text{PMT}}$

Now press the $\boxed{\text{FV}}$ key, and an FV of $563.71 is displayed.

Example 2:

What is the PV of the same annuity?

Leave data in calculator, but enter 0 as the FV to override, then press $\boxed{\text{PV}}$, and you get a PV of $421.24.

Annuities Due

Each payment of an annuity due occurs at the beginning of the period instead of at the end, as with a regular annuity. In essence, each payment is shifted back one period. To analyze an annuity due press $\boxed{\text{G}}$ $\boxed{\text{BEG / END}}$. The word "BEGIN" appears on the screen. Now the HP analyzes the cash flows based on beginning of period payments. Change back to end mode by pressing $\boxed{\text{G}}$ $\boxed{\text{BEG / END}}$.

Interest Conversion

The following equation is used to convert a nominal rate to an effective rate.

$$EAR = \left[1 + \frac{k_{NOM}}{m}\right]^m - 1$$

Given: k_{NOM} = 10% and m = 12 payments / year, we can solve for the annual effective rate using this formula. However, this formula is programmed into your calculator and it is much easier to convert to the effective rate using the calculator:

10 [G] [NOM %]

12 [G] [P/YR]

    [G] [EFF %]   = 10.47% is displayed on the screen.

Now switch back to 1 payment per year: [1] [G] [P/YR]

Cash Flow Operations

Example 1: Uneven Cash Flows

Assume the following cash flows:

What is the PV of these CFs?

First, clear, the calculator and make sure that P/YR is set to 1.

0   **CFⱼ**   Sets CF_0 equal to 0.

50   **CFⱼ**   Sets CF_1 equal to 50. On the next entry, hold down the CF_j

100   **CFⱼ**   key, and you can see that you just entered CF_2.

150   **CFⱼ**

200   **CFⱼ**

The CFs from the time line are entered. Now enter the interest rate.

10   **I/YR**

At this point the HP knows the cash flows, the number of periods, and the interest rate. To find the PV, press   **G**   **NPV**   to get PV = NPV = \$377.40.

Example 2: Embedded Annuities

We have these cash flows, which contain embedded annuities:

What's the PV?

Clear all, and make sure that the calculator is set to 1 P/YR.

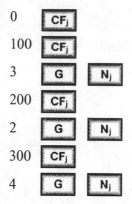

0 [CFj]

100 [CFj]

3 [G] [Nj]

200 [CFj]

2 [G] [Nj]

300 [CFj]

4 [G] [Nj]

Now the calculator knows the cash flows. Thus, enter the interest rate:

10 [I/YR]

Now press [G] [NPV] to get PV = NPV = $1,099.94.

To check your entries:

[RCL] 0 to see CF_0.

[RCL] [CFj] to see the first CF entry.

[RCL] [G] [Nj] to see how many times CF_1 is repeated, etc.

Example 3: The Internal Rate of Return of an Investment (IRR)

Assume that we invest $1,000 today (t = 0) and then expect to receive an uneven set of cash flows. Here is the CF time line:

What rate of return will we earn? Enter the following:

| 1000 | G +/- | CLEAR ALL |
| | | CF_j |

1000 [G] [+/-] [CLEAR ALL] [CF_j]
300 [CF_j]
400 [CF_j]
200 [CF_j]
600 [CF_j]
[G] [IRR] =16.71%

You can also determine the NPV of the investment. Leave data entered and then enter the opportunity cost interest rate, say 8 percent. To find NPV press:

8 [I/YR]
[G] [NPV]

The NPV of $220.50 is displayed. Thus, the PV of the cash inflows exceeds the cost of the investment by $220.50.

Statistical Calculations

The HP can also be used for several types of statistical calculations.

Mean and Standard Deviation

Year	Sales
1999	$150
2000	95
2001	260

What is the mean (average) and standard deviation (σ) of sales over the 3 years?

Use the $\boxed{\Sigma+}$ key to enter data:

$$\boxed{G} \quad \boxed{\text{CLEAR ALL}}$$

$$150 \quad \boxed{\Sigma+}$$

$$95 \quad \boxed{\Sigma+}$$

$$260 \quad \boxed{\Sigma+}$$

Determine the mean and standard deviation by simply pressing

$\boxed{G}$ $\boxed{\bar{x}, \bar{y}}$ The mean equals $168.33

$\boxed{G}$ $\boxed{S_x, S_y}$ The standard deviation is $84.01. S_x and S_y ar sample standard deviations. σ_x and σ_y refer to population statistics.

Linear Regression

Beta coefficients can be calculated by using the HP's linear regression capabilities. The X (independent variable) and Y (dependent variable) values must be entered in the proper sequence, where the X data is on the horizontal axis (**market**) and Y data is on the vertical axis (**stock**).

Year	Market (k_M)	Stock (k_J)
1	23.8%	38.6%
2	-7.2%	-24.7%
3	6.6%	12.3%
4	20.5%	8.2%
5	30.6%	40.1%

Enter the data as follows:

The value –8.92 is y when x = 0, or k_j when k_M = 0, which is the vertical axis intercept of the regression line.

The value displayed, 1.60, is the *beta* coefficient.

Amortization

The HP can also be used to calculate amortization schedules.

Example:

Determine the interest and principal paid each year and the balance at the end of each year on a three-year $1,000 amortizing loan which carries an interest rate of 10 percent. The payments are due annually.

First, check payments/year and be sure it is set to 1. Now perform the following steps:

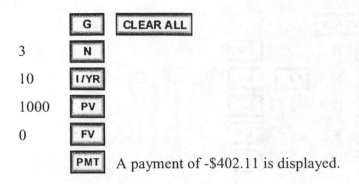

This is the amortization schedule corresponding to the loan.

Period	Beg. Bal.	Payment	Interest	Princ. Repmt.	Ending Bal.
1	1000.00	402.11	100.00	302.11	697.89
2	697.89	402.11	69.79	332.33	365.56
3	365.56	402.11	36.56	365.56	0.00

With the data still entered in the TVM menu, do the following:

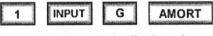

    "PER 1-1" is displayed.

| = | Press to see "PRIN", which is the amount paid towards principal over the first year. Write it into a table as -302.11.

| = | Press to see "INT" = -100.00. This is the amount paid towards interest over the first year. Write it into the table.

| = | Press to see "BAL" = 697.89, the balance at the end of the first year.

G **AMORT**

    "PER 2-2" is displayed.

| = | -332.33 is the principal paid in Year 2.

[=] -69.79 is the interest paid in Year 2.

[=] 365.56 is the ending balance at end of Year 2.

[G] [AMORT]

"PEr 3-3" is displayed.

[=] -365.56 is the principal repayment in Year 3.

[=] -36.56 is the interest paid in Year 3.

[=] 0.00 is the balance at end of Year 3.

See the manual for an explanation of how to do monthly amortization.

Next, with the data still in the calculator, do the following:

[1] [INPUT] [3] [G] [AMORT]

"PER 1-3" is displayed.

[=] Hold down to see Int, then release and -206.34 displayed. This is the total interest paid over Years 1 to 3.

[=] Hold down to see Prin, then release and –1,000.00 is displayed. This is the total repayment of principal over Years 1 to 3.

[=] Hold down to see Bal, then release and 0.00 is displayed. This is the remaining balance.

Hewlett-Packard 12C Tutorial

To begin, look at the face of the calculator. Every key (except the arithmetic function keys in the far right column and the five keys on the bottom left row) has two or three functions: each key's primary function is noted in white on the key itself, while each key's secondary function is noted in gold above the key or in blue on the lower face of the key. To use the function on the key, simply press the key. To access the gold function above each key, first press the gold $\boxed{f}$ key, which we will call the "gold shift" key, and then press the desired function key. (Note that the gold shift key is near the lower left corner of the calculator keyboard.) To access the blue function on the bottom of each key, first press the blue $\boxed{g}$ key, which we will call the "blue shift" key, and then press the desired function. (The blue shift key is located just to the right of the gold shift key.)

Turning the Calculator On and Off

To turn on the calculator, press $\boxed{ON}$.

Note that the ON key is on the lower left corner of the keyboard—the face of the key has a white "ON". Also, we will designate keys throughout this tutorial by the use of small boxes, as above. To conserve the battery, the calculator turns itself off about 10 minutes after your last keystroke.

To turn the calculator off, press $\boxed{ON}$ again.

Also, note that pressing the gold shift key places a little "f" in the lower left corner of the display. Pressing the blue shift key places a little "g" at the bottom of the display. Press the $\boxed{CLX}$ key and the symbol goes away. The shift keys are toggle keys that switch back and forth between the "regular" and the "gold" or "blue" functions. They are like the typewriter shift key. After you press the "gold" (or "blue") key, look only at gold (or blue) writing.

Note that the calculator has a continuous memory, so turning it off does not affect any data stored in the calculator.

Clearing the Calculator

Clearing the calculator is very important, since unwanted data in memory can result in improper calculations, and hence wrong answers. It is best to get into the habit of automatically clearing memory before starting a calculation. Occasionally, you may purposely want to save data, but, in general, you will be entering all new data, so starting with a clear memory is the safest approach.

There are four different levels of clearing data:

[f] [REG] clears all memory and the display.

[CLX] clears the entire display, but not the memory.

[f] [FIN] clears the financial register but not the display.

[f] [Σ] clears the statistics register and the display.

Note that the keys above are designated as CLEAR keys on the face of the calculator.

Changing the Display

Enter 5555.5555.

To change decimals from 2 to 4, press [f] [4]. 5,555.5555 is displayed.

To change from 4 places to 2, press [f] [2]. 5,555.56 is displayed. (Rounding is automatic.)

We usually set the display to 2 places, which is especially convenient when working with dollars and percentages. However, we often use 4 places when dealing with interest rates and rates of return that are entered as decimals.

Time Value of Money (TVM)

The TVM keys are located on the top row of the keyboard.

[n] [i] [PV] [PMT] [FV]

In general, TVM problems involve four variables—three are known and the fourth is unknown.

Lump Sums

To begin, we consider TVM calculations with single (lump) sums. In this situation, we do not use the PMT key, so be sure to either clear all, which sets the payment (PMT) equal to 0, or enter 0 as the PMT when entering the input data. If you know any three variables, you can find the value of the fourth.

Example 1:

What is the FV of $100 after 3 years if the interest rate is 26 percent? First, clear with 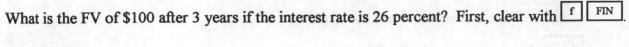.

Next, enter the data.

3 [n]

26 [i]

100 [PV]

0 [PMT] (Optional if registers are cleared.)

To determine the FV simply press [FV] and the FV of -$200.04 is displayed.

The HP is programmed so that if the PV is + then the FV is displayed as - and vice versa, because the HP assumes that one is an inflow and the other is an outflow. When entering both PV and FV, one must be entered as negative and the other positive.

Example 2:

What is the PV of $500 due in 5 years if the interest rate is 10 percent? Clear first and then enter the following data:

5 [n]

10 [i]

0 [PMT] (Optional if registers are cleared.)

500 [FV]

Pressing the [PV] key reveals that $310.46 will grow to $500 in 5 years at a 10 percent rate.

Example 3:

Assume a bond can be purchased today for $200. It will return $1,000 after 14 years. The bond pays no interest during its life. What rate of return would you earn if you bought the bond?

14 $\boxed{n}$

200 $\boxed{CHS}$ $\boxed{PV}$ (The $\boxed{CHS}$ key changes the sign.)

0 $\boxed{PMT}$

1000 $\boxed{FV}$

Simply press the $\boxed{i}$ key and the HP calculates the rate of return to be 12.18 percent.

Remember that the HP is programmed so that if the PV is + then the FV is displayed as - and vice versa, because the HP assumes that one value is an inflow and other is an outflow. Also note that the negative sign is placed on the 200 PV entry by pressing the key marked "CHS" for change sign.

Now suppose you learn that the bond will actually cost $300. What rate of return will you earn?

Override the -200 by entering 300 $\boxed{CHS}$ $\boxed{PV}$, then press $\boxed{i}$ to get 8.98 percent. If you pay more for the bond, you earn less on it. The important thing, though, is that you can do "what if" analyses with the calculator.

Now press $\boxed{ON}$ to turn off the calculator. Then turn on the calculator $\boxed{ON}$. The display still shows 8.98. The memory is not erased. What was on the screen when you turned the calculator off returns when you turn it back on. Now press $\boxed{CLX}$. What was on the screen is gone, but press $\boxed{RCL}$ $\boxed{n}$ to get N = 14. The other memory registers also retain information unless you press $\boxed{f}$ $\boxed{FIN}$.

Ordinary Annuities

Example 1:

What is the FV of an annuity of $100 paid at the end of each year for 5 years if the interest rate equals 6 percent?

5   n

6   i

0   PV

100   CHS   PMT

Now press the FV key, and an FV of $563.71 is displayed.

Example 2:

What is the PV of the same annuity?

Leave data in calculator, but enter 0 as the FV to override, then press PV to get $421.24.

Annuities Due

Each payment of an annuity due occurs at the beginning of the period instead of at the end as with a regular annuity. In essence, each payment is shifted back one period. To analyze annuities due press g BEG. The word "BEGIN" appears on the screen. Now the HP analyzes the cash flows based on beginning of period payments. Change back to end mode by pressing g END.

Interest Conversion

The following equation is used to convert a nominal rate to an effective rate.

$$ EAR = \left[1 + \frac{k_{Nom}}{m}\right]^m - 1. $$

Given: $k_{Nom} = 10\%$ and $m = 12$ payments/year,

$$EAR = \left[1 + \frac{0.10}{12}\right]^m - 1 = (1.0083)^{12} - 1 = 1.1047 - 1 = 0.1047 = 10.47\%.$$

However, it's much easier to convert the nominal rate using the calculator:

First, clear the financial register, $\boxed{f}\ \boxed{FIN}$.

10	$\boxed{ENTER}$	

12	$\boxed{n}$ $\boxed{\div}$ $\boxed{i}$	

$\boxed{CHS}$ $\boxed{PMT}$ $\boxed{FV}$ 10.47% shows on the screen.

Cash Flow Operations

We can also find the PV, FV, and IRR (rate of return) of a series of unequal cash flows.

Example 1: Uneven Cash Flows

Assume the following cash flows:

What is the PV of these CFs?

First clear the HP's financial register, $\boxed{f}\ \boxed{FIN}$.

0	$\boxed{g}$ $\boxed{CF_o}$	Sets CF_0 equal to 0.
50	$\boxed{g}$ $\boxed{CF_j}$	Sets CF_1 equal to 50.
100	$\boxed{g}$ $\boxed{CF_j}$	
150	$\boxed{g}$ $\boxed{CF_j}$	
200	$\boxed{g}$ $\boxed{CF_j}$	

The CFs from the time line are entered. Now enter the interest rate:

10 $\boxed{i}$

At this point the HP knows the cash flows, the number of periods, and the interest rate. To find the PV, press $\boxed{f}$ $\boxed{\text{NPV}}$ to get PV = NPV = \$377.40.

Example 2: Embedded Annuities

We have these cash flows, which contain embedded annuities:

What's the PV?

Clear the HP, $\boxed{f}$ $\boxed{\text{FIN}}$.

0 $\boxed{g}$ $\boxed{\text{CF}_0}$

100 $\boxed{g}$ $\boxed{\text{CF}_j}$

3 $\boxed{g}$ $\boxed{\text{N}_j}$

200 $\boxed{g}$ $\boxed{\text{CF}_j}$

2 $\boxed{g}$ $\boxed{\text{N}_j}$

300 $\boxed{g}$ $\boxed{\text{CF}_j}$

4 $\boxed{g}$ $\boxed{\text{N}_j}$

Now the HP knows the cash flows. Thus, enter the interest rate:

10 $\boxed{i}$

Now press $\boxed{f}$ $\boxed{\text{NPV}}$ to get PV = NPV = \$1,099.94.

To check your entries:

RCL 0		to see CF_0.
RCL 1		to see first CF entry, 100.00 in this example.
1 [n] [RCL] [g] [N_j]		to see how many times CF_1 is repeated. The display shows that the first CF occurs three consecutive times.

Example 3: The Rate of Return Offered by an Investment (IRR)[1]

Assume that we invest $1,000 now (t = 0) and then expect to receive an uneven set of cash flows. Here is the CF time line:

What rate of return will we earn? Enter the following:

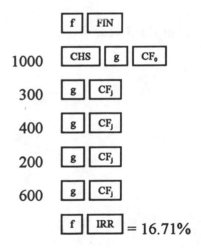

f [FIN]

1000 [CHS] [g] [CF_0]

300 [g] [CF_j]

400 [g] [CF_j]

200 [g] [CF_j]

600 [g] [CF_j]

[f] [IRR] = 16.71%

---

[1]If a negative CF occurs at the end of a project's life, then the HP may give an error message, indicating that there are two IRRs. Enter data, then enter 10 [ENTER] and then [RCL] [g] [R/S] to get the first IRR. Then enter a large percentage, such as 100 [ENTER] and then [RCL] [g] [R/S] to find the other IRR. You might have to experiment with "guesses" to locate the two IRRs.

You can also determine the NPV of the investment. Leave data entered and then enter the opportunity cost interest rate, say 8 percent. To find NPV press:

8 | i | | f | | NPV |

The NPV of $220.50 is displayed. Thus, the PV of the cash inflows exceeds the cost of the investment by $220.50.

Statistical Calculations

The HP can also be used for several types of statistical calculations.

Mean and Standard Deviation (σ)

Year	Sales
1994	$150
1995	95
1996	260

What's the mean (average) and standard deviation (σ) of sales over the 3 years?

Use the Σ+ key to enter data:

	f		Σ		Clears the statistical register.
150	Σ+		A number 1 is displayed.
95	Σ+		A number 2 is displayed.
260	Σ+		A number 3 is displayed.

Determine the mean and standard deviation by simply pressing

| g | | x̄ | The mean equals $168.33.

| g | | s | The standard deviation is $84.01. S is the sample standard deviation.

Linear Regression

Beta coefficients can be calculated by using the HP's linear regression capabilities. The X (independent variable) and Y (dependent variable) values must be entered in the proper sequence, where X data is on the horizontal axis (**market**) and Y data is on the vertical axis (**stock**).

Year	Market (k_M)	Stock (k_j)
1	23.8%	38.6%
2	-7.2	-24.7
3	6.6	12.3
4	20.5	8.2
5	30.6	40.1

Enter the data as follows:

| f | Σ |

Note: The order in which the data is entered is very important. The Y value (k_j) must be entered before the X value (k_M).

38.6 | ENTER | 23.8 | Σ+ |

24.7 | CHS | ENTER | 7.2 | CHS | Σ+ |

12.3 | ENTER | 6.6 | Σ+ |

8.2 | ENTER | 20.5 | Σ+ |

40.1 | ENTER | 30.6 | Σ+ |

0 | g | ŷ,r | The value -8.92 is y when x = 0, or k_j when k_M = 0, which is the *vertical axis intercept*.

| STO | 0 | Stores the value of the Y intercept for use in calculating the slope (beta).

0 | g | x̂,r | 5.57 is the value of x when y = 0.

| RCL | 0 | CHS | x≷y | ÷ | The value displayed, 1.60, is the slope coefficient, or the *beta coefficient*.

Amortization

The HP can also be used to calculate amortization schedules.

Example:

Determine the interest and principal paid each year and the balance at the end of each year on a three-year $1,000 amortizing loan which carries an interest rate of 10 percent. The payments are due annually.

Perform the following steps:

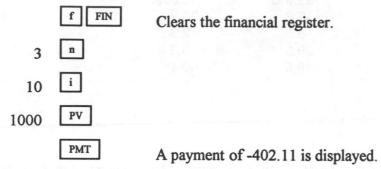

	f FIN	Clears the financial register.		
3	n			
10	i			
1000	PV			
	PMT	A payment of -402.11 is displayed.		

This is the amortization schedule corresponding to the loan.

	Beg. Bal.	Payment	Interest	Princ. Repmt.	Ending Bal.
1	1,000.00	402.11	100.00	302.11	697.89
2	697.89	402.11	69.79	332.32	365.57
3	365.57	402.11	36.56	365.55	.02

With the data still entered in the TVM menu, do the following:

1 [f] [AMORT] Tells the calculator that you want to amortize the first payment only. The display shows -100.000, which is the interest payment during the first year. Write it into a table as 100.00.

[X≷Y] The display shows -302.11. This is the repayment of principal in the first year. Write it in the table.

[RCL] [PV] The display shows 697.89. This is the remaining principal balance at the end of the first year. Write it down.

1 [f] [AMORT] This tells the calculator that you want to amortize the next payment only. The number of payments keyed in just before [f] [AMORT] is taken to be the payments following any that have been already amortized. Thus, keying in 1 at this step moved you into the second payment period.

-69.79 is the interest paid in Year 2.

X≷Y		-332.32 is the principal paid in Year 2.
RCL	PV	365.57 is the ending balance at end of Year 2.
1	f	AMORT	-35.56 is the interest paid in Year 3.
X≷Y		-365.55 is the principal repayment in Year 3.
RCL	PV	0.02 is the balance at end of Year 3.

See the manual for an explanation of how to do monthly amortization.

Next, with the data still in the calculator, do the following:

1000 PV   This returns the calculator to the original principal balance of $1,000.

3 f AMORT   Tells the calculator that you want to amortize the first three payments together. In this example there are only 3 payments, but that is not always the case. The display shows -206.35. This is the total interest paid over Years 1 to 3.

X≷Y   -999.98 is the total repayment of principal over Years 1 to 3.

RCL PV   0.02 is the remaining balance.

Hewlett-Packard 17BII Tutorial

To begin, look at the face of the calculator. Most keys on the 17BII have two functions: a key's primary function is noted in white on the key itself, while the key's secondary function is noted in gold above the key. To use the function on the key, simply press the key. To access the gold function above each key, first press the key with the solid gold face, which we will call the "gold shift" key, and then press the desired function key. (Note that the gold shift key is near the lower left corner of the calculator keyboard.)

Turning the Calculator On and Off

To turn on the calculator, press $\boxed{\text{CLR}}$.

Note that the ON key is on the lower left corner of the keyboard—the face of the key has a white "CLR," while the word "ON" appears below the key. Also, we will designate keys throughout this tutorial by the use of small boxes, as above. To conserve the battery, the calculator turns itself off about 10 minutes after your last keystroke.

To turn the calculator off, press $\blacksquare$ $\boxed{\text{OFF}}$.

Here we are using the solid black square to represent the gold shift key. Thus, the keystrokes to turn the calculator off are (1) press the gold shift key, and (2) then press the CLR key. Note that the word "OFF" appears above the CLR key in gold. Thus, by pressing the gold shift key first, we are activating the gold function above the CLR key, which is the off function. Also, note that pressing the gold shift key places a little "up arrow" symbol in the upper left corner of the display. Press the gold shift key again and the symbol goes away. The $\blacksquare$ key is a toggle key that switches back and forth between the "regular" and the "gold" functions. $\blacksquare$ is like the typewriter shift key. After you press $\blacksquare$, look only at the gold writing.

Note that the calculator has a continuous memory, so turning it off does not affect any data stored in the calculator.

The Menu System

The HP17BII differs from many calculators in that it uses a menu system. To access the main menu, press $\blacksquare$ $\boxed{\text{MAIN}}$. The display shows five menu choices: FIN, BUS, SUM, TIME, and SOLVE. To access one of the menu choices, press the arrowhead key directly below the appropriate choice. To illustrate, press the arrowhead key directly below FIN. (We will designate this operation by $\boxed{\text{FIN}}$. Thus, a shaded box means press one of the arrowhead keys rather than one of the regular keys.) Now a new set of menu choices appears. Press [TVM] to get into the time value of money menu. To get back to the main menu, either press ▉[MAIN] or press [EXIT] a number of times until the menu items stop changing.

Clearing the Calculator

To clear the calculator's memory, press ▉[CLEAR DATA].

Clearing the calculator is very important, since unwanted data in memory can result in improper calculations, and hence wrong answers. It is best to get into the habit of automatically clearing memory before starting a calculation. Occasionally, you may purposely want to save data, but, in general, you will be entering all new data, so starting with a clear memory is the safest approach.

There are three different levels of clearing data:

▉[CLEAR DATA] clears all memory and the display.

[CLR] clears the entire display, but not the memory.

[←] clears numbers on the display one at a time if you made a mistake entering data.

Changing the Display

To change the number of decimal places from 2 to 4, press [DSP] [FIX] [4] [INPUT]. Now press 5555.5555 [INPUT]. 5,555.5555 is displayed.

Note that the calculator display itself is often used to designate calculator functions. When this occurs, we shade the box as above. To invoke the function displayed, press the arrowhead key directly below the function.

To change from 4 places to 2, press [DSP] [FIX] [2] [INPUT]. Now press 5555.5555 [INPUT]. 5,555.56 is displayed. (Rounding is automatic.)

We usually set the display to 2 places, which is especially convenient when working with dollars and percentages. However, we often use 4 places when dealing with interest rates and rates of return that are entered as decimals.

To control the brightness of the display, hold down CLR and press + or - .

Periods per Year Setting

One important setting that can cause problems is the periods per year setting. To check the current setting, first press ▮ MAIN to get the main menu, and then press FIN TVM . The display shows the setting for periods/year. The calculator comes pre-set at 12 periods per year, that is, it assumes calculations will be done on a monthly basis. However, the problems in finance textbooks generally use 1 period/year. To change to 1/year:

1) From the main menu, press FIN TVM OTHER 1 P/YR .
2) Return to the main menu by pressing EXIT three times or ▮ MAIN .

Time Value of Money (TVM)

To enter the time value of money menu, do the following:

From the main menu, press FIN TVM .

In general, TVM problems involve four variables—three are known and the fourth is unknown.

Lump Sums

To begin, we consider TVM calculations with single (lump) sums. In this situation, we do not have payments, so be sure to either press CLEAR DATA , which sets the payment (PMT) equal to 0, or enter 0 for the PMT. If you know any three variables, you can find the value of the fourth.

Example 1:

What is the FV of $100 after 3 years if the interest rate is 26 percent? First, clear with ▮ CLEAR DATA and enter the following data:

3 [N]

26 [I%YR]

100 [PV]

0 [PMT] (Optional if registers are cleared.)

Next, press [FV] and the future value of -$200.04 is displayed.

The HP is programmed so that if the PV is + then the FV is displayed as - and vice versa, because the HP assumes that one is an inflow and the other is an outflow. If you are entering both PV and FV, one must be entered as negative and the other positive.

Example 2:

What is the PV of $500 due in 5 years if the interest rate is 10 percent? Clear data first and then enter the following:

5 [N]

10 [I%YR]

0 [PMT] (Optional if registers are cleared.)

500 [FV]

Next, press [PV] and the present value of -$310.46 is displayed. Thus, $310.46 will grow to $500 in 5 years at a 10 percent rate.

Example 3:

Assume a bond can be purchased today for $200. It will return $1,000 after 14 years. The bond pays no interest during its life. What rate of return would you earn if you bought the bond?

Next, press and a rate of return of 12.18 percent is displayed.

Remember to press $\boxed{+/-}$ to convert the 200 to -200 because the purchase of the bond is a cash outflow!

Now suppose you learn that the bond will actually cost $300. What rate of return will you earn?

Override the -200 by simply entering 300 $\boxed{+/-}$ $\boxed{\text{PV}}$ and then press $\boxed{\text{I\%YR}}$ to get 8.98 percent. If you pay more for the bond, you earn less on it. The important thing, though, is that you can do "what if" analyses with the calculator.

Ordinary Annuities

Now we will use the PMT key, and either the PV or the FV key, depending on whether we want to find the PV or the FV of the annuity.

Example 1:

What is the FV of an annuity of $100 paid at the end of each year for 5 years if the interest rate equals 6 percent?

5 N

6 I%YR

0 PV

100 +/- PMT

Now press the FV key, and an FV of $563.71 is displayed.

Example 2:

What is the PV of the same annuity?

Leave data in calculator, but enter 0 as the FV to override, then press PV to get $421.24.

Annuities Due

Each payment of an annuity due occurs at the beginning of the period instead of at the end as with a regular annuity. In essence, each payment is shifted back one period. To analyze annuities due press FIN TVM OTHER BEG. The words "BEGIN MODE" appear on the screen. Now the HP analyzes the cash flows based on beginning of period payments. Change back to end mode by pressing END. To get back to the TVM menu press EXIT.

Interest Conversion

The following equation is used to convert a nominal rate to an effective rate.

$$EAR = \left[1 + \frac{k_{Nom}}{m}\right]^m - 1.$$

Given: $k_{Nom} = 10\%$ and $m = 12$ payments/year,

$$EAR = \left[1 + \frac{0.10}{12}\right]^m - 1 = (1.0083)^{12} - 1 = 1.1047 - 1 = 0.1047 = 10.47\%.$$

This formula is fine, however, the calculator can be used to convert the rates much faster.

From the main menu press [FIN] [ICNV] [PER].

Now, enter 12 and then press [P] to compound 12 times per year.

To enter 10 percent as the nominal rate, press 10 [NOM %].

Now, to determine the effective rate simply press [EFF %] and 10.47 percent is displayed.

Cash Flow Operations

The HP is useful for finding the PV, FV, and IRR (rate of return) of a series of unequal cash flows.

Example 1: Uneven Cash Flows

Assume the following cash flows:

What is the PV of these CFs? Clear the memory by pressing [■] [CLEAR DATA].

You should also clear any previously entered cash flow lists by pressing [FIN] [CFLO] [■] [CLEAR DATA] [YES].

Now, press [#T?] until "#TIMES PROMPTING: OFF" is displayed because each cash flow is different than the one before it and thus occurs only one time. There is no need for the HP to prompt you for the number of times that a particular cash flow occurs since each one is different than the one before it.

The screen should now display "FLOW(0)=?". Next, enter the following:

0	INPUT	This enters 0 as the cash flow at time 0.
50	INPUT	This enters 50 as the CF_1.
100	INPUT	This enters 100 as the CF_2.
150	INPUT	This enters 150 as the CF_3.
200	INPUT	This enters 200 as the CF_4.

After all the cash flows have been entered, press EXIT to return to the menu. Select CALC and "NPV, NUS, NFV NEED I%" is displayed.

Now enter the 10 percent interest rate by pressing 10 I%.

At this point the HP knows the cash flows, the number of periods, and the interest rate. To find the NPV, press NPV to get PV = NPV = \$377.40.

Example 2: Embedded Annuities

Assume the following cash flows, which contain embedded annuities or groups of equal, consecutive cash flows:

What's the PV?

Clear the previously entered cash flow lists by pressing FIN CFLO ■ CLEAR DATA YES from the main menu.

Now enter #T? until "#TIMES PROMPTING: ON" is displayed. After each cash flow is entered the calculator will prompt you for the number of times that cash flow occurs. This feature saves you from having to enter identical, consecutive cash flows one by one. If each cash flow is different than the one before it (see previous example), then the "#TIMES PROMPTING" can be turned off.

The screen should now display "FLOW(0)=?".

Next enter the cash flows.

0	INPUT	This enters 0 as CF_0.
100	INPUT	This enters 100 as the CF_1.
3	INPUT	This tells the HP that the $100 CF occurs three consecutive times.
200	INPUT	This enters 200 as the CF_2.
2	INPUT	This tells the HP that the $200 CF occurs two consecutive times.
300	INPUT	This enters 300 as the CF_3.
4	INPUT	This tells the HP that the $300 CF occurs four consecutive times.

After all the cash flows have been entered, press EXIT to return to the menu. Select CALC and "NPV, NUS, NFV NEED I%" is displayed.

Now enter the 10 percent interest rate by pressing 10 I%.

At this point the HP knows the cash flows, the number of periods, and the interest rate. To find the NPV, press NPV to get PV = NPV = $1,099.94.

Lastly, the ▲ and ▼ keys can be used to view your cash flow list entries. First, exit to the menu that looks like this:

CALC	INSR	DELET	NAME	GET	#T?

Then simply use the ▲ and ▼ keys to view the cash flow entries.

Example 3: The Rate of Return Offered by an Investment (IRR)[1]

Assume that we invest $1,000 now (t = 0) and then expect to receive an uneven set of cash flows.

---

[1]If a negative CF occurs at the end of a project's life, then the HP may give an error message, indicating that there are two IRRs. Enter data, then enter 10 STO IRR to get the first IRR. Then enter a large percentage, such as 100 STO IRR to find the other IRR. You might have to experiment with "guesses" to locate the two IRRs.

Here is the CF time line:

0	1	2	3	4
-1000	300	400	200	600

What rate of return will we earn?

Clear the previously entered cash flow lists by pressing . Now press [#T?] until the "#TIMES PROMPTING" is turned off.

Now enter the cash flows as follows:

1000 [+/-] [INPUT]

300 [INPUT]

400 [INPUT]

200 [INPUT]

600 [INPUT]

After all the cash flows have been entered, press [EXIT] to return to the menu. Select [CALC] and "NPV, NUS, NFV NEED I%" is displayed.

Now enter the 10 percent interest rate by pressing 10 [I%].

At this point the HP knows the cash flows, the number of periods, and the interest rate.

To find the IRR, press [IRR%] to get IRR = 16.71%.

You can also determine the NPV of the investment. Leave data entered and then enter the opportunity cost interest rate, say 8 percent. To find NPV press:

8 [I%] [NPV]

The NPV of $220.50 is displayed. Thus, the PV of the cash inflows exceeds the cost of the investment by $220.50.

Statistical Calculations

The HP can also be used for several types of statistical calculations.

Mean and Standard Deviation (σ)

Year	Sales
1994	$150
1995	95
1996	260

What's the mean (average) and standard deviation (σ) of sales over the 3 years?

The first step is to enter the data into a sum list. From the main menu press [SUM].

Clear any previously entered sum lists by next pressing:

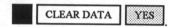 [CLEAR DATA] [YES].

"ITEM(1)=?" is displayed.

Enter the sales data into the sum list as follows:

150 [INPUT]

95 [INPUT]

260 [INPUT]

Now press [EXIT] to return to the menu and then press [CALC] to display the following menu:

[TOTAL] [MEAN] [MEDN] [STDEV] [RANG] [MORE]

Press [MEAN] and the mean of $168.33 is displayed.

Press [STDEV] and the standard deviation of $84.01 is displayed.

Linear Regression

Beta coefficients can be calculated by using the HP's linear regression capabilities. The X (independent variable) and Y (dependent variable) values must be entered in the proper sequence, where the X data is on the horizontal axis (**market**) and Y data is on the vertical axis (**stock**).

Year	Market (k_M)	Stock (k_j)
1	23.8%	38.6%
2	-7.2	-24.7
3	6.6	12.3
4	20.5	8.2
5	30.6	40.1

Enter the data as follows.

To clear any previously entered list, from the main menu, press:

First we must create two sum lists: one for the x-values and one for the y-values. Each list must have the same number of items.

To create a sum list for the x-values do the following:

Enter the five X variables:

23.8 | INPUT |

7.2 | +/- | | INPUT |

6.6 | INPUT |

20.5 | INPUT |

30.6 | INPUT |

Now we must store this list under a name before we create another sum list for the Y variables. Store the X variable sum list as follows:

The HP now asks you to input a name for the sum list. We will name the list "X" by pressing:

| WXYZ | X | INPUT | Of course you could have named the list any name that sufficiently describes the contents of the list (market return) such as KM or MKRT.

We have just created a sum list names "X", which contains the five X variables.

The display now shows "ITEM(6)=?" but we need to create a sum list for the Y variables starting with Item(1). To create a new sum list for Y, start a new list as follows:

| GET | *NEW | This tells the HP to start a new sum list.

Now simply enter the Y variables and name the list "Y" just as you did for the X variables above.

Next, press | CALC | MORE | FRCST |.

At this time, the HP asks you to select the X variable from the lists we created:

Press | X | to select the list named "X" and press | Y | to select the list named "Y" as the Y variable.

Next, we must select the curve-fitting model we want to use by pressing:

| MORE | MODL | LIN |.

To calculate the curve-fitting results, press

| CORR | Calculates the correlation coefficient, 0.91.

| M | Calculates the slope coefficient, or the beta coefficient, 1.60.

| B | Calculates the Y-intercept, -8.92.

That's all there is to it!

Amortization

The amortization menu calculates the loan balance after payments are made and calculates the amount of the payments applied toward interest and principal.

Example:

Assume a $1,000 loan at 10 percent with annual payments is amortized over 3 years. Create an amortization schedule for this loan.

From the main menu, press [FIN] [TVM] [OTHER] [1] [P/YR] to set payments/year equal to 1.

Exit to the TVM menu and enter the following:

3 [N]

10 [I%YR]

1000 [PV]

Next, to calculate the payment press [PMT] and the loan payment of $402.11 is displayed.

Now press [OTHER] [AMRT] to enter the amortization menu.

Key in the number of payments for which to calculate the amortization schedule:

1 [#P]   We entered 1 because we want to determine the principal paid, interest paid, and remaining balance after each payment is made.

Now press:

[INT] Displays interest paid in first year: "INTEREST = -100.0".

[PRIN] Displays principal paid in first year: "PRINCIPAL = -302.11".

[BAL] Displays balance at end of first year: "BALANCE = 697.89".

To calculate the amortization schedule for the second year, press [NEXT] [INT] [PRIN] [BAL].

Repeat for the third year.

The amortization table you create should contain these results. If not, try it again.

	Beg. Bal.	Payment	Interest	Princ. Repmt.	Ending Bal.
1	1,000.00	402.11	100.00	302.11	697.89
2	697.89	402.11	69.79	332.32	365.57
3	365.57	402.11	36.56	365.55	.02

Sharp EL-733A Tutorial

To begin, look at the face of the calculator. Almost every key on the EL-733A has two functions: each key's primary function is noted on the key itself, while each key's secondary function is noted in reddish-brown above the key. To use the function on the key, simply press the key. To access the function above each key, first press the yellow key with "2ndF" printed on it, which we will call the "2nd function" key, and then press the desired function key. (Note that the 2nd function key is located at the upper left corner of the calculator keyboard.)

Turning the Calculator On and Off

To turn on the calculator, press $\boxed{\text{C-CE}}$. To turn off the calculator, press $\boxed{\text{OFF}}$.

Note that the ON and OFF keys are in the upper right corner of the keyboard. Also, we will designate keys throughout this tutorial by the use of small boxes, as above. To conserve the battery, the calculator turns itself off about 10 minutes after your last keystroke.

Also, note that pressing the 2nd function key places a little "2ndF" symbol in the upper left corner of the display. Press the 2nd function key again and the symbol goes away. The $\boxed{\text{2ndF}}$ key is a toggle key that switches back and forth between the "regular" and the "2nd" functions. $\boxed{\text{2ndF}}$ is like the typewriter shift key. After you press $\boxed{\text{2ndF}}$, look only at the reddish-brown writing above the keys.

Note that the calculator has a continuous memory, so turning it off does not affect any data stored in the calculator, but will erase any number showing on the screen.

Clearing the Calculator

Three of the most commonly used methods of clearing data are presented below:

$\boxed{\text{2ndF}}$ $\boxed{\text{CA}}$ Clears all the memory registers associated with a particular mode (normal, FIN, or STAT).

$\boxed{\text{C-CE}}$ Clears the entire display, but not the memory.

$\boxed{\rightarrow}$ Clears numbers on the display one at a time if you made a mistake entering data.

Review your owner's manual for other methods of clearing information.

Clearing the calculator is very important, since unwanted data in memory can result in improper calculations, and hence wrong answers. It is best to get into the habit of automatically clearing memory before starting a calculation. Occasionally, you may purposely want to save data, but, in general, you will be entering all new data, so starting with a clear memory is the safest approach.

Changing the Display

To change decimals from 2 to 4, press $\boxed{\text{2ndF}}$ $\boxed{\text{TAB}}$ $\boxed{4}$. 0.0000 is displayed.

To change from 4 places to 2, press $\boxed{\text{2ndF}}$ $\boxed{\text{TAB}}$ $\boxed{2}$. 0.00 is displayed.

We usually set the display to 2 places, which is especially convenient when working with dollars and percentages. However, we often use 4 places when dealing with interest rates and rates of return that are entered as decimals.

Changing the Mode

The calculator has three calculation modes: NORMAL, FIN (financial), and STAT (statistics). The mode of the calculator dictates the type of calculations that can be performed. When working financial problems, you will typically use the FIN mode, while statistical problems normally will be handled in STAT mode. Modes are indicated in the display as follows: a box showing "FIN" indicates finance mode, a box showing "STAT" indicates statistics mode, and no box appears when in the normal mode. To change modes, simply press, $\boxed{\text{2ndF}}$ $\boxed{\text{MODE}}$. The calculator rotates through the modes from normal to finance to statistics to normal.

Time Value of Money (TVM)

The TVM keys are located on the third row from the top of the keyboard.

$\boxed{\text{n}}$ $\boxed{\text{i}}$ $\boxed{\text{PV}}$ $\boxed{\text{FV}}$ $\boxed{\text{PMT}}$

To enter the time value of money mode do the following:

Press $\boxed{\text{2ndF}}$ $\boxed{\text{MODE}}$ repeatedly until the 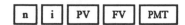 indicator appears in the display.

In general, TVM problems involve four variables—three are known and the fourth is unknown.

Lump Sums

To begin, we consider TVM calculations with single (lump) sums. In this situation, we do not use the PMT key, so be sure to either clear all, which sets the payment (PMT) equal to 0, or enter 0 as the PMT when entering the input data. If you know any three variables, you can find the value of the fourth.

Example 1:

What is the FV of $100 after 3 years if the interest rate is 26 percent? First, clear with ⌐2ndF⌐ ⌐CA⌐.

Next, enter the data.

$$3 \quad \boxed{n}$$
$$26 \quad \boxed{i}$$
$$100 \quad \boxed{PV}$$
$$0 \quad \boxed{PMT} \quad \text{(Optional if registers are cleared.)}$$

To determine the FV simply press ⌐COMP⌐ ⌐FV⌐ and the FV of -$200.04 is displayed. (COMP is the key framed in black near the upper left corner.)

The EL-733A is programmed so that if the PV is + then the FV is displayed as - and vice versa, because the EL-733A assumes that one is an inflow and the other is an outflow. When entering both PV and FV, one must be entered as negative and the other as positive.

Example 2:

What is the PV of $500 due in 5 years if the interest rate is 10 percent? Clear first and then enter the following data.

$$5 \quad \boxed{n}$$
$$10 \quad \boxed{i}$$
$$0 \quad \boxed{PMT} \quad \text{(Optional if registers are cleared.)}$$
$$500 \quad \boxed{FV}$$

Pressing the ⌐COMP⌐ ⌐PV⌐ key reveals that $310.46 will grow to $500 in 5 years at a 10 percent rate.

Example 3:

Assume a bond can be purchased today for $200. It will return $1,000 after 14 years. The bond pays no interest during its life. What rate of return would you earn if you bought the bond?

Simply press the COMP i key and the HP calculates the rate of return to be 12.18%.

Remember that the EL-733A is programmed so that if the PV is + then the FV is displayed as - and vice versa, because the EL-733A assumes that one is an inflow and other is an outflow. Also, note that the negative sign is placed on the 200 PV entry by pressing the key marked "+/-".

Now suppose you learn that the bond will actually cost $300. What rate of return will you earn?

Override the -200 by entering 300 +/- PV , then press COMP i to get 8.98 percent. If you pay more for the bond, you earn less on it. The important thing, though, is that you can do "what if" analyses with the calculator.

Now do nothing except press OFF to turn off the calculator. Then turn on the calculator C-CE . The display shows 0.00. Is the memory erased? Not completely. What was on the screen is gone, but press 2ndF RCL n to see that the N = 14 entry is still in the calculator's memory.

Ordinary Annuities

Example 1:

What is the FV of an annuity of $100 paid at the end of each year for 5 years if the interest rate equals 6 percent?

5   [n]

6   [i]

0   [PV]

100   [+/-] [PMT]

Now press the [COMP] [FV] key, and an FV of $563.71 is displayed.

Example 2:

What is the PV of the same annuity?

Leave data in calculator, but enter 0 as the FV to override, then press [COMP] [PV] to get $421.24.

Annuities Due

Each payment of an annuity due occurs at the beginning of the period instead of at the end as with a regular annuity. In essence, each payment is shifted back one period. To analyze annuities due press [BGN]. The symbol "BGN" appears in the upper right corner of the display. Now the EL-733A analyzes the cash flows based on beginning of period payments. Change back to end mode by pressing [BGN] again.

Interest Conversion

The following equation is used to convert a nominal rate to an effective rate.

$$EAR = \left[1 + \frac{k_{Nom}}{m} \right]^m - 1.$$

Given: $k_{Nom} = 10\%$ and m = 12 payments/year,

$$EAR = \left[1 + \frac{0.10}{12} \right]^m - 1 = (1.0083)^{12} - 1 = 1.1047 - 1 = 0.1047 = 10.47\%.$$

However, it's much easier to convert the nominal rate using the calculator.

Before beginning this procedure it is important to note that another name for the nominal rate is the annual percentage rate (APR). In fact, the EL-733A uses the term APR for the nominal interest rate. Thus, the keystrokes required to calculate the above effective rate for 12 compounding periods would be as follows:

> 12 | 2ndF | | →EFF | 10 | = |

The effective rate of 10.47% is displayed on the screen.

If you were given the effective rate and wished to convert it to an APR (nominal rate), the key strokes for 12 compounding periods would be as follows:

> 12 | 2ndF | | →APR | 10.4713 | = |

The nominal rate of 10.00 percent is displayed on the screen.

Cash Flow Operations

We can also find the PV, FV, and IRR (internal rate of return) of a series of unequal cash flows.

Example 1: Uneven Cash Flows

Assume the following cash flows:

What is the PV of these CFs?

First clear any previous cash flow or TVM analyses by pressing [2ndF] [CA]. Next, enter the cash flows:

0	[CFi]	Sets CF_0 equal to 0 and moves to CF_1.
50	[CFi]	Sets CF_1 equal to 50 and so on.
100	[CFi]	
150	[CFi]	
200	[CFi]	

The CFs from the time line are entered. Now enter the interest rate.

10 [i]

At this point the EL-733A knows the cash flows, the number of periods, and the interest rate. To find the PV, press [COMP] [NPV] to get PV = NPV = $377.40.

Example 2: Embedded Annuities

We have these cash flows, which contain embedded annuities:

What's the PV?

First clear any previous cash flow analyses, [2ndF] [CA]. Next, enter the cash flows:

0	[CFi]	Sets CF_0 equal to 0 and moves to CF_1.
3	[2ndF] [Ni]	Tells the calculator that the *following* CF will occur three consecutive times.
100	[CFi]	Sets the first three CFs equal to 100.
2	[2ndF] [Ni]	
200	[CFi]	
4	[2ndF] [Ni]	
300	[CFi]	

Now the EL-733A knows the cash flows. Thus, enter the interest rate:

10 [i]

At this point the EL-733A knows the cash flows, the number of periods, and the interest rate. To find the PV, press [COMP] [NPV] to get PV = NPV = $1,099.94.

To check your entries:

Press [2ndF] [RCL] [1] to see that the amount of the first group of CFs is $100.00 each. You can now check the frequency of this CF group by pressing [2ndF] [RCL] [2ndF] [Ni]. This $100.00 cash flow occurs 3 consecutive times.

Example 3: The Rate of Return Offered by an Investment (IRR)[1]

Assume that we invest $1,000 now (t = 0) and then expect to receive an uneven set of cash flows. Here is the CF time line:

What rate of return will we earn?

First clear any previous cash flow analyses, | 2ndF | | CA |. Next, enter the cash flows:

1000		+/-		CFi		Sets CF_0 equal to -1000 and moves to CF_1.
300		CFi		Sets CF_1 equal to 300 and moves to CF_2.
400		CFi		
200		CFi		
600		CFi		

Now the EL-733A knows the cash flows. Thus, simply press | COMP | | IRR | and the IRR of 16.71 percent is displayed.

You can also determine the NPV of the investment. Leave data entered and then enter the opportunity cost interest rate, say 8 percent. To find NPV press

8 | i | | COMP | | NPV |

The NPV of $220.50 is displayed. Thus, the PV of the cash inflows exceeds the cost of the investment by $220.50.

---

[1]If a negative CF occurs at the end of a project's life, or if a sequence of cash flows has two or more sign changes, there may be multiple IRR solutions. The calculator displays the IRR closest to zero. However, the displayed solution has no financial meaning. Thus, you should use caution in making investment decisions based on an IRR computed for a cash flow stream with more than one sign change. When you are solving very complex cash flow problems, the calculator may not be able to find IRR, even if a solution exists. When this is the case, the calculator displays *E*. An error can be cleared by pressing the | C-CE | key.

Statistical Calculations

The EL-733A can also be used for several types of statistical calculations.

Mean and Standard Deviation (σ)

Year	Sales
1994	$150
1995	95
1996	260

What's the mean (average) and standard deviation (σ) of sales over the 3 years?

First, put the calculator into the Statistics mode by pressing $\boxed{\text{2ndF}}$ $\boxed{\text{MODE}}$ until the $\boxed{\text{STAT}}$ indicator shows on the display. Then clear any previous data entries, $\boxed{\text{2ndF}}$ $\boxed{\text{CA}}$. Next, enter the data:

150 $\boxed{\text{M+}}$ — This enters 150 as the data entry and tells the calculator it occurs one time. Note that $\boxed{\text{DATA}}$ is the meaning of the $\boxed{\text{M+}}$ key when the calculator is in the statistics (STAT) mode.

95 $\boxed{\text{M+}}$ — This enters 95 as the second data entry and tells the calculator it occurs one time.

260 $\boxed{\text{M+}}$ — This enters 260 as the third data entry and tells the calculator it occurs one time.

Determine the mean by simply pressing the following:

$\boxed{\text{2ndF}}$ $\boxed{\overline{\text{X}}}$ — The mean equals $168.33.

Determine the standard deviation by pressing the following:

$\boxed{\text{2ndF}}$ $\boxed{\text{S}_x}$ — The standard deviation is $84.01. S_x and S_y are sample standard deviations. σ_x and σ_y refer to population statistics.

Linear Regression

Beta coefficients can be calculated by using the EL-733A's linear regression capabilities. The X (independent variable) and Y (dependent variable) values must be entered in the proper sequence, where the X data is on the horizontal axis (**market**) and Y data is on the vertical axis (**stock**).

Year	Market (k_m)	Stock (k_j)
1	23.8%	38.6%
2	-7.2	-24.7
3	6.6	12.3
4	20.5	8.2
5	30.6	40.1

First, put the calculator into the Statistics mode by pressing [2ndF] [MODE] until the [STAT] indicator shows on the display. The clear any previous data entries, [2ndF] [CA]. Next, enter the data as follows:

23.8 [RM]		This enters 23.8 as the first X variable. (The [RM] key in the STAT mode is the [(x, y)] key.)
38.6 [M+]		This enters 38.6 as the first Y variable.
7.2 [+/-] [RM]		This enters -7.2 as the second X variable.
24.7 [+/-] [M+]		This enters -24.7 as the second Y variable.
6.6 [RM]		This enters 6.6 as the third X variable.
12.3 [M+]		This enters 12.3 as the third Y variable.
20.5 [RM]		This enters 20.5 as the fourth X variable.
8.2 [M+]		This enters 8.2 as the fourth Y variable.
30.6 [RM]		This enters 30.6 as the fifth X variable.
40.1 [M+]		This enters 4.1 as the fifth Y variable.

Determine the intercept by pressing [2ndF] [a]. The display shows that "a," which is the *vertical axis intercept*, is equal to -8.92. To find the slope simply press [2ndF] [b]. The display shows that "b" is equal to 1.60, which is the slope coefficient and the *beta coefficient*.

Amortization

The EL-733A can also be used to calculate amortization schedules.

Example:

Determine the interest and principal paid each year and the balance at the end of each year on a three-year $1,000 amortizing loan which carries an interest rate of 10 percent. The payments are due annually.

Press | 2ndF | | MODE | repeatedly until the | FIN | indicator comes on the display screen. Then clear any previous data entries, | 2ndF | | CA |.

Now perform the following steps:

3		n	
10		i	
1000		PV	
		COMP		PMT	A payment of -$402.11 is displayed.

Now, since all the information about the loan is stored in the TVM register, we can use the amortization functions to generate an amortization schedule for the loan.

Determine the principal and interest paid in each payment, and the balance remaining after each payment by doing the following steps:

1 $\boxed{\text{AMRT}}$ Entering 1 tells the calculator we want to examine the first year. The display shows that PRN = -302.11. Thus, out of the first $402.11 payment, $302.11 went toward paying off the principal portion of the loan.

$\boxed{\text{AMRT}}$ The display shows that INT = -100.00. Thus, out of the first $402.11 payment, $100.00 was payment of interest.

$\boxed{\text{AMRT}}$ The display shows that BAL = 697.89. Thus, after making the first $402.11 payment, the principal balance you to be paid is $697.89.

2 $\boxed{\text{AMRT}}$ The 2 moves to the second year. The display shows that the principal repayment is Year 2 is PRN = -332.33.

$\boxed{\text{AMRT}}$ The interest payment is INT = -69.79.

$\boxed{\text{AMRT}}$ The remaining balance is BAL = 365.56.

3 $\boxed{\text{AMRT}}$ For Year 3, the principal repayment is PRN = -365.56.

$\boxed{\text{AMRT}}$ The interest payment is INT = -36.56.

$\boxed{\text{AMRT}}$ The remaining balance is BAL = 0.

Here is the complete amortization table:

	Beg. Bal.	Payment	Interest	Princ. Repmt.	Ending Bal.
1	1,000.00	402.11	100.00	302.11	697.89
2	697.89	402.11	69.79	332.33	365.56
3	365.56	402.11	36.56	365.56	0.00

Texas Instruments BAII PLUS Tutorial

To begin, look at the face of the calculator. Almost every key on the BAII PLUS has two functions: each key's primary function is noted on the key itself, while each key's secondary function is noted in white above the key. To use the function on the key, simply press the key. To access the white function above each key, first press the gray key with "2nd" printed on it, which we will call the "2nd shift" key, and then press the desired function key. (Note that the 2nd shift key is near the upper left corner of the calculator keyboard.)

Turning the Calculator On and Off

To turn on the calculator, press $\boxed{\text{ON/OFF}}$. To turn off the calculator, press $\boxed{\text{ON/OFF}}$.

Note that the "ON/OFF" key is on the upper right corner of the keyboard. Also, we will designate keys throughout this tutorial by the use of small boxes, as above. To conserve the battery, the calculator turns itself off about 10 minutes after your last keystroke.

Also, note that pressing the 2nd shift key places a little "2nd" symbol in the upper left corner of the display. Press the 2nd shift key again and the symbol goes away. The $\boxed{\text{2nd}}$ key is a toggle key that switches back and forth between the "regular" and the "2nd" functions. $\boxed{\text{2nd}}$ is like the typewriter shift key. After you press $\boxed{\text{2nd}}$, look only at the white writing above the keys.

Note that the calculator has a continuous memory, so turning it off does not affect any data stored in the calculator, but it will erase any number showing on the screen.

Clearing the Calculator

Five of the most commonly used methods of clearing data are presented below:

$\boxed{\text{2nd}}$ $\boxed{\text{MEM}}$ $\boxed{\text{2nd}}$ $\boxed{\text{CLR WORK}}$ clears all 10 memory locations and the display.

$\boxed{\text{2nd}}$ $\boxed{\text{QUIT}}$ $\boxed{\text{2nd}}$ $\boxed{\text{CLR TVM}}$ clears the TVM worksheet.

$\boxed{\text{2nd}}$ $\boxed{\text{CLR WORK}}$ clears worksheets other than the TVM worksheet.

$\boxed{\text{CE/C}}$ clears the entire display, but not the memory.

$\boxed{\rightarrow}$ clears numbers on the display one at a time if you made a mistake entering data.

Review your owner's manual for other methods of clearing information.

Clearing the calculator is very important, since unwanted data in memory can result in improper calculations, and hence wrong answers. It is best to get into the habit of automatically clearing memory before starting a calculation. Occasionally, you may purposely want to save data, but, in general, you will be entering all new data, so starting with a clear memory is the safest approach.

Changing the Display

To change decimals from 2 to 4, press [2nd] [FORMAT] [4] [ENTER] [2nd] [QUIT]. 0.0000 is displayed.

To change from 4 places to 2, press [2nd] [FORMAT] [2] [ENTER] [2nd] [QUIT]. 0.00 is displayed.

We usually set the display to 2 places, which is especially convenient when working with dollars and percentages. However, we often use 4 places when dealing with interest rates and rates of return that are entered as decimals.

Periods per Year Setting

One important setting that can cause problems is the periods per year setting. To check the current setting, press [2nd] [P/Y]. The display shows the setting for periods/year. The calculator comes pre-set at 12 periods per year, that is, it assumes calculations will be done on a monthly basis. However, finance textbook problems generally use 1 period/year. To change to 1/year:

Press [2nd] [P/Y] 1 [ENTER] [2nd] [QUIT].

Now the calculator is set to assume 1 period/year. To confirm this setting, press [2nd] [P/Y] [2nd] [QUIT]. Unless needed for other work, we generally leave the calculator setting at 1 period per year.

Time Value of Money (TVM)

The TVM keys are located on the third row from the top of the keyboard.

[N] [I/Y] [PV] [PMT] [FV]

In general, TVM problems involve four variables—three are known and the fourth is unknown.

Lump Sums

To begin, we consider TVM calculations with single (lump) sums. In this situation, we do not use the PMT key, so be sure to either press [2nd] [CLR TVM], which sets the payment (PMT) equal to 0, or enter 0 as the PMT when entering the input data. If you know any three variables, you can find the value of the fourth.

Example 1:

What is the FV of $100 after 3 years if the interest rate is 26 percent? First, clear with [2nd] [CLR TVM].

Next, enter the data.

3 [N]

26 [I/Y]

100 [PV]

0 [PMT]   (Optional if registers are cleared.)

To determine the FV simply press [CPT] [FV] and the FV of -$200.04 is displayed.

The BAII PLUS is programmed so that if the PV is + then the FV is displayed as - and vice versa, because the BAII PLUS assumes that one is an inflow and the other is an outflow. When entering both PV and FV, one must be entered as negative and the other as positive.

Example 2:

What is the PV of $500 due in 5 years if the interest rate is 10 percent? Clear first and then enter the following data.

5 [N]

10 [I/Y]

0 [PMT]   (Optional if registers are cleared.)

500 [FV]

Pressing the [CPT] [PV] key reveals that $310.46 will grow to $500 in 5 years at a 10 percent rate.

Example 3:

Assume a bond can be purchased today for $200. It will return $1,000 after 14 years. The bond pays no interest during its life. What rate of return would you earn if you bought the bond?

Simply press the [CPT] [I/Y] key and the BAII PLUS calculates the rate of return to be 12.18%.

Remember that the BAII PLUS is programmed so that if the PV is + then the FV is displayed as - and vice versa because the BAII PLUS assumes that one is an inflow and the other is an outflow.

Now suppose you learn that the bond will actually cost $300. What rate of return will you earn?

Override the -200 by entering 300 [+/-] [PV], then press [CPT] [I/Y] to get 8.98 percent. If you pay more for the bond, you earn less on it. The important thing, though, is that you can do "what if" analyses with the calculator.

Now do nothing except press [ON/OFF] to turn off the calculator. Then turn on the calculator [ON/OFF]. The display shows 0.00. Is the memory erased? Not completely. What was on the screen is gone, but press [RCL] [N] to get N = 14.

Ordinary Annuities

Example 1:

What is the FV of an annuity of $100 paid at the end of each year for 5 years if the interest rate equals 6 percent?

5 [N]

6 [I/Y]

0 [PV]

100 [+/-] [PMT]

Now press the [CPT] [FV] key, and an FV of $563.71 is displayed.

Example 2:

What is the PV of the same annuity?

Leave data in calculator, but enter 0 as the FV to override, then press [CPT] [PV] to get $421.24.

Annuities Due

Each payment of an annuity due occurs at the beginning of the period instead of at the end as with a regular annuity. In essence, each payment is shifted back one period. To analyze annuities due press [2nd] [BGN] [2nd] [SET] [CE/C]. "BGN" appears on the screen and in the upper right corner of the display. Now the BAII PLUS analyzes the cash flows based on beginning of period payments. Change back to end mode by pressing [2nd] [BGN] [2nd] [SET] [CE/C].

Interest Conversion

The following equation is used to convert a nominal rate to an effective rate.

$$EAR = \left[1 + \frac{k_{Nom}}{m}\right]^m - 1.$$

Given: $k_{Nom} = 10\%$ and $m = 12$ payments/year,

$$EAR = \left[1 + \frac{0.10}{12}\right]^m - 1 = (1.0083)^{12} - 1 = 1.1047 - 1 = 0.1047 = 10.47\%.$$

However, it's much easier to convert the nominal rate using the calculator.

First, we need to set the calculator to 12 payments per year:

| 2nd | | I CONV | | ↑ | 12 | ENTER |

| ↓ | 10 | ENTER |

| ↓ | | CPT |

The effective rate of 10.47 percent is displayed on the screen.

Cash Flow Operations

Example 1: Uneven Cash Flows

We can also find the PV, FV, and IRR (internal rate of return) of a series of unequal cash flows.

Assume the following cash flows:

What is the PV of these CFs?

First clear the BAII PLUS and make sure that periods/year is set equal to 1.

Enter the cash flow worksheet by pressing $\boxed{\text{CF}}$ then clear any previous cash flow analyses, $\boxed{\text{2nd}}$ $\boxed{\text{CLR WORK}}$. Next, enter the cash flows:

0 $\boxed{\text{ENTER}}$ $\boxed{\downarrow}$ Sets CF_0 equal to 0 and moves to CF_1.

50 $\boxed{\text{ENTER}}$ $\boxed{\downarrow}$ Sets CF_1 equal to 50 and moves to frequency of occurrence of CF_1.

1 $\boxed{\text{ENTER}}$ $\boxed{\downarrow}$ Tells calculator that the $50 CF occurs only once.

100 $\boxed{\text{ENTER}}$ $\boxed{\downarrow}$

1 $\boxed{\text{ENTER}}$ $\boxed{\downarrow}$

150 $\boxed{\text{ENTER}}$ $\boxed{\downarrow}$

1 $\boxed{\text{ENTER}}$ $\boxed{\downarrow}$

200 $\boxed{\text{ENTER}}$ $\boxed{\downarrow}$

1 $\boxed{\text{ENTER}}$

The CFs from the time line are entered. Now enter the interest rate.

$\boxed{\text{NPV}}$ 10 $\boxed{\text{ENTER}}$ $\boxed{\downarrow}$

At this point the BAII PLUS knows the cash flows, the number of periods, and the interest rate. To find the PV, press $\boxed{\text{CPT}}$ to get PV = NPV = $377.40.

Example 2: Embedded Annuities

We have these cash flows, which contain embedded annuities:

What's the PV?

Clear, set P/YR = 1 if changed.

First enter the cash flow worksheet by pressing [CF] then clear any previous cash flow analyses, [2nd] [CLR WORK]. Next, enter the cash flows:

0	[ENTER] [↓]		Sets CF_0 equal to 0 and moves to CF_1.
100	[ENTER] [↓]		Sets CF_1 equal to 100 and moves to frequency of occurrence of CF_1.
3	[ENTER] [↓]		Tells calculator that the $100 CF occurs three consecutive times.
200	[ENTER] [↓]		
2	[ENTER] [↓]		
300	[ENTER] [↓]		
4	[ENTER]		

Now the BAII PLUS knows the cash flows. Thus, enter the interest rate:

[NPV] 10 [ENTER] [↓].

At this point the BAII PLUS knows the cash flows, the number of periods, and the interest rate. To find the PV, press [CPT] to get PV = NPV = $1,099.94.

To check your entries:

[CF] then use the up and down arrow keys to view each cash flow.

Example 3: The Rate of Return Offered by an Investment (IRR)[1]

Assume that we invest $1,000 now (t = 0) and then expect to receive an uneven set of cash flows. Here is the CF time line:

```
    0       1       2       3       4
    |       |       |       |       |
  -1000    300     400     200     600
```

What rate of return will we earn?

First enter the cash flow worksheet by pressing [CF] then clear any previous cash flow analyses, [2nd] [CLR WORK]. Next, enter the cash flows:

1000 [+/-] [ENTER] [↓]   Sets CF_0 equal to -1,000 and moves to CF_1.

300 [ENTER] [↓] [↓]   Sets CF_1 equal to -1000 and moves to frequency of occurrence of CF_1. The second [↓] tells calculator that the $300 CF occurs only once.[2]

400 [ENTER] [↓] [↓]

200 [ENTER] [↓] [↓]

600 [ENTER] [↓] [↓]

Now the BAII PLUS knows the cash flows. Thus, simply press [IRR] [CPT] and the IRR of 16.71 percent is displayed.

---

[1] If a negative CF occurs at the end of a project's life, or if a sequence of cash flows has two or more sign changes, there may be multiple IRR solutions. The calculator displays the IRR closest to zero. However, the displayed solution has no financial meaning. Thus, you should use caution in making investment decisions based on an IRR computed for a cash flow stream with more than one sign change. When you are solving very complex cash flow problems, the calculator may not be able to find IRR, even if a solution exists. When this is the case, the calculator displays *Error 7* (iteration limit exceeded).

[2] If you do not enter a value for frequency after you enter the cash flow value, the calculator assumes a value of 1; however, the down arrow key must be pressed again before entering the next cash flow.

You can also determine the NPV of the investment. Leave data entered and then enter the opportunity cost interest rate, say 8 percent. To find NPV press

| I/YR | 8 | ENTER | ↓ | CPT |

The NPV of $220.50 is displayed. Thus, the PV of the cash inflows exceeds the cost of the investment by $220.50.

Statistical Calculations

The BAII PLUS can also be used for several types of statistical calculations.

Mean and Standard Deviation (σ)

Year	Sales
1994	$150
1995	95
1996	260

What's the mean (average) and standard deviation (σ) of sales over the 3 years?

First select the data-entry portion of the statistics worksheet by pressing [2nd] [DATA] then clear any previous data entries, [2nd] [CLR WORK]. Next, enter the data:

150 [ENTER] [↓] [↓]   This enters 150 as the data entry and tells the calculator there is no Y-variable associated with the X variable.

95 [ENTER] [↓] [↓]   This enters 95 as the second data entry and tells the calculator there is no Y-variable associated with the X variable.

260 [ENTER] [↓] [↓]   This enters 260 as the third data entry and tells the calculator there is no Y-variable associated with the X variable.

Now select the statistical calculation portion of the statistics worksheet by pressing [2nd] [STAT] then clear any previous statistical entries, [2nd] [CLR WORK].

"LIN" should now be displayed on the screen. Keep pressing [2nd] then [SET] until "1-V" (one variable calculation method) is displayed. Press the down arrow key three times to view (1) sample size, n, (2) mean, $\bar{x}$, and (3) standard deviation, Sx. The mean equals $168.33. The standard deviation is $84.01.

Linear Regression

Beta coefficients can be calculated by using the BAII PLUS's linear regression capabilities. The X (independent variable) and Y (dependent variable) values must be entered in the proper sequence, where the X data is on the horizontal axis (**market**) and Y data is on the vertical axis (**stock**).

Year	Market (k_m)	Stock (k_j)
1	23.8%	38.6%
2	-7.2	-24.7
3	6.6	12.3
4	20.5	8.2
5	30.6	40.1

First select the data-entry portion of the statistics worksheet by pressing $\boxed{\text{2nd}}$ $\boxed{\text{DATA}}$ then clear any previous statistical entries, $\boxed{\text{2nd}}$ $\boxed{\text{CLR WORK}}$.

Next, enter the data as follows:

23.8	$\boxed{\text{ENTER}}$ $\boxed{\downarrow}$	This enters 23.8 as the first X variable.
38.6	$\boxed{\text{ENTER}}$ $\boxed{\downarrow}$	This enters 38.6 as the first Y variable.
7.2	$\boxed{\text{+/-}}$ $\boxed{\text{ENTER}}$ $\boxed{\downarrow}$	This enters -7.2 as the second X variable.
24.7	$\boxed{\text{+/-}}$ $\boxed{\text{ENTER}}$ $\boxed{\downarrow}$	This enters -24.7 as the second Y variable.
6.6	$\boxed{\text{ENTER}}$ $\boxed{\downarrow}$	This enters 6.6 as the third X variable.
12.3	$\boxed{\text{ENTER}}$ $\boxed{\downarrow}$	This enters 12.3 as the third Y variable.
20.5	$\boxed{\text{ENTER}}$ $\boxed{\downarrow}$	This enters 20.5 as the fourth X variable.
8.2	$\boxed{\text{ENTER}}$ $\boxed{\downarrow}$	This enters 8.2 as the fourth Y variable.
30.6	$\boxed{\text{ENTER}}$ $\boxed{\downarrow}$	This enters 30.6 as the fifth X variable.
40.1	$\boxed{\text{ENTER}}$ $\boxed{\downarrow}$	This enters 40.1 as the fifth Y variable.

Now select the statistical calculation portion of the statistics worksheet by pressing [2nd] [STAT] then clear any previous statistical entries, [2nd] [CLR WORK].

"LIN" should now be displayed on the screen. Keep pressing [↓] until "a =" appears on the screen. This is the value of the y-intercept of the regression line. Press [↓] one more time and "b =" appears one the screen. This is the value of the slope of the regression line. If you press [↓] one more time, "r =" appears on the screen. This is the value of the correlation coefficient of the regression line. (The intercept value is -8.92, the slope value is 1.60, and the correlation coefficient is 0.91.)

Clear the calculator by pressing [2nd] [DATA] [2nd] [CLR WORK].

Amortization

The BAII PLUS can also be used to calculate amortization schedules. First, clear the TVM registers by pressing [2nd] [QUIT] [2nd] [CLR TVM].

Example:

Determine the interest and principal paid each year and the balance at the end of each year on a three-year $1,000 amortizing loan which carries an interest rate of 10 percent. The payments are due annually.

First, check payments/year and be sure it's 1. ([2nd] [P/Y] [2nd] [QUIT])

Now perform the following steps:

3 [N]

10 [I/Y]

1000 [PV]

[CPT] [PMT] A payment of -402.11 is displayed.

Now we will use the amortization worksheet to generate an amortization schedule for the loan:

| 2nd | AMORT | 2nd | CLR WORK |

Enters the Amort worksheet and clears any old contents.

| ↓ | 1 | ENTER |

Ending period set at 1 because we want to view the amortization information for each and every payment.

Now just use the down arrow key to view the balance after the payment as well as the interest and principal portions of the first payment.

To view the results for the second payment, press | ↓ | to move to "P1," press | CPT | and use the down arrow key to view the ending balance after the payment is made as well as the interest and principal portions of the second payment.

Repeat for the third and last payment.

This is the amortization schedule corresponding to the loan.

	Beg. Bal.	Payment	Interest	Princ. Repmt.	Ending Bal.
1	1,000.00	402.11	100.00	302.11	697.89
2	697.89	402.11	69.79	332.32	365.57
3	365.57	402.11	36.56	365.55	.02

Spreadsheet Tutorial

By

Laura A. Eakins[1] and Stanley G. Eakins[2]
East Carolina University

---

[1] Department of Decision Sciences
[2] Department of Finance

INTRODUCTION

The Information Age is upon us. In 1957, for the first time in history, white collar workers outnumbered blue collar workers, signaling the beginning of a new era, a period where information would rule supreme. More jobs now deal with the gathering, processing, and disseminating of information than ever before. Along with this new age came rapid advancements in computer hardware and software and, therefore, tremendous changes in financial management. Microcomputers more powerful than mainframes of a few years ago are now affordable to any business, and new and improved software makes it easy to do things that were not feasible several years ago.

Because so many businesses rely on computers, it is crucial that anyone with a serious interest in financial management develop at least a minimal level of spreadsheet literacy. Most employers realize that students with solid computer skills are a valuable asset to any business. Today, students who are not comfortable with microcomputers, spreadsheets, word processing, and inter-computer communications are not very marketable.

The first electronic spreadsheet program was called Visicalc (short for visible calculator) and was developed in 1979 by two students at Harvard University. The program was written to run on an Apple II personal computer. Because it was the first of its kind, this program caused widespread interest in the new and growing world of personal computers. It is estimated that Visicalc alone was responsible for the sale of over 20,000 Apple computers.

Since the days of Visicalc, many computer programs such as Excel, Lotus 1-2-3, and QuattroPro have been developed for working with spreadsheets. A spreadsheet is simply a tool used for quantitative analysis. An electronic spreadsheet program is the computerized equivalent of the old manual system of recording information on a ledger sheet. The purpose is to record data in a logical, organized manner.

A spreadsheet consists of a grid or matrix of rows and columns. The intersection of a row and a column forms a cell which can hold numbers, text, or a formula. The spreadsheet's usefulness comes from its ability to recalculate results as you change the contents of other cells. The user need not do these calculations by hand or on a calculator anymore. Rather, an electronic spreadsheet should be used with formulas inserted into some cells. In this way, the spreadsheet recalculates the desired values automatically. Every time the content of a cell changes, any formulas relating to that cell are automatically recalculated.

In these instances, the spreadsheet is set up to perform "what if" analysis. What if sales are below the expected level? What if costs of manufacturing go up? With a properly constructed spreadsheet using formulas, any data changes will result in a recalculation of the spreadsheet, and the impact of the change on net income is shown immediately. For this reason, spreadsheets are used extensively in financial planning and analysis, instances that involve large amounts of numerical data.

GETTING STARTED

In this tutorial, basic information will be presented on using spreadsheets. The tutorial is based on Microsoft Excel, version 7.0. Where applicable, guidelines will also be noted for using Lotus 1-2-3 for Windows, version 5.0. These guidelines will be inserted in the form of "Lotus Tip" boxes. By comparing the two programs, you will find that they are remarkably similar since both are Windows based. We will only note significant differences between the two. If a Lotus Tip does not appear in the text, assume that Excel and Lotus function in a similar manner.

Before you can do any work with your spreadsheet, you have to load the program into your computer's memory. The location of the Excel or Lotus icon will depend on the organization of your system. In Windows 3.1, if you are using Program Manager as the main shell, locate the Excel or Lotus icon and double click on that icon. In Windows95 click on the Start button in the bottom left corner of your screen, then choose **P**rograms and then Microsoft Excel or Lotus 1-2-3.

> **Lotus Tip**
> In Lotus the program will present a dialog box asking whether you wish to open a new spreadsheet or work on an existing spreadsheet. If you choose to work on an existing sheet, the program then loads that sheet for you. If you choose to start a new spreadsheet, you are presented with another dialog box that offers you a choice of several worksheet templates. Press the enter key if you wish to accept the default Lotus setting, which opens a plain worksheet.

IDENTIFYING PARTS OF THE WORKSHEET

The following page shows the Excel screen as it will first appear when you enter the program. The various parts of the screen have been identified. We will discuss each part in detail in the sections that follow.

> **Lotus Tip**
> The appendix shows the Lotus screen. Lotus looks slightly different from Excel. These differences will be noted in the appendix.

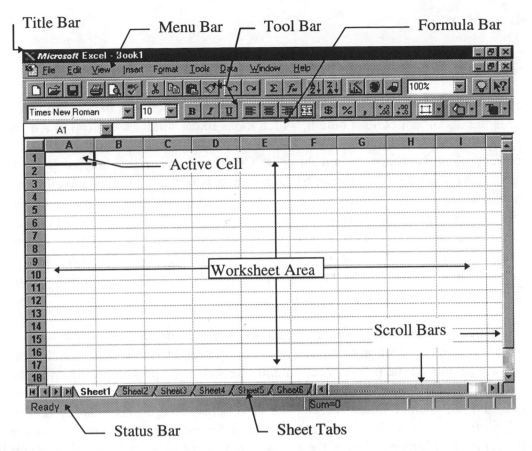

The Title Bar

The title bar is located at the top of the Excel screen. In the far left corner of the title bar is the application control button, which in Excel 7.0 looks like an "X," short for Excel. Clicking once on this button causes a menu to drop down that controls the application window. This menu allows choices for moving the window, changing its size, and closing the program, as well as the ability to switch to or run other programs. Clicking twice on this button closes the program. To the right of the application control button is the name of the program and the workbook that is currently active.

The right side of the title bar has three buttons. From left to right, the first button is the minimize button. It will reduce the window down to a box on the taskbar at the bottom of the Windows screen where it is still active, but out of the way. The second button is the restore button. Clicking on it will restore the window back to a smaller window that does not occupy the whole screen. This allows the Windows desktop screen to be visible also. Once you have clicked on the restore button, this new smaller window has the maximize button as the second button instead of the restore button. The maximize button expands the window, causing it to occupy the entire screen again. The third button looks like an "X" and closes the program.

The Menu Bar

| | File | Edit | View | Insert | Format | Tools | Data | Window | Help | | | _ | 🗗 | ✕ |

The main menu bar in Excel is located directly under the title bar. On the far left side of the menu bar is the document control button, which looks like a small "x" on top of a document. Clicking once on this button causes the same menu to drop down that is present when you click on the application control button above it. Clicking twice on this button closes the worksheet. The remainder of the menu bar allows access to the nine menus available in the program. Choosing one of these menu items leads you to the options that are available under that particular item. There are two ways to select a menu: click on the menu of choice with the mouse, or use the Alt key in combination with the underlined letter in the menu name. For example, to choose the **F**ile menu, either click with the mouse on the word "**F**ile" or press Alt-F on the keyboard. Either method will lead to the **F**ile menu dropping down, allowing you to make another choice.

Notice that when you are working in the Windows program, menus stay visible on the screen until you either make a selection or cancel the menu by pressing the Esc key or clicking the mouse anywhere outside the menu. These menus are said to be persistent, meaning they remain on the screen. While the menu is visible, using the arrow keys or the mouse to highlight individual menu choices will cause a short help message to be displayed at the bottom of the Excel screen. This help message describes what action the highlighted menu selection performs. Memorization of the menus is really not necessary. By simply scrolling through the menus in this manner, you will eventually learn where items are located. Once you locate the option that you want to select, simply click the left mouse button or press Enter.

Sometimes when you choose a menu, some of the selections in the drop down menu beneath it will be displayed in a light gray color instead of black. This means that these options are not available for selection at this time. For example, if you have not cut or copied a cell, the **P**aste option from the **E**dit menu has nothing to paste, so it is grayed indicating that it is not available as an option at this time. Once you have cut or copied some data, the paste function will be shown in black type, indicating that the option is available to you to use. Remember, only the menu options displayed in black may be selected.

Some menu selections will be followed by a series of three periods. This indicates that once that menu item is selected, a dialog box will appear and more information will be needed. For example, if you select the **P**rint option from the **F**ile menu, the program will need more information from you as to what part of the spreadsheet you want to print, how many copies, and so forth. When a menu selection is not followed by three periods, it means that selecting that option will carry out the task and no dialog box will appear.

The last item on the menu bar is the "**H**elp" option. The Help Menu can guide you through the steps necessary to accomplish any task using Microsoft Excel. For example, suppose you don't know how to put a border around text in your spreadsheet. Choose **H**elp, Microsoft

Excel **H**elp Topics, then choose Index and type the word "border" in the box provided. From there, the program will instruct you on how to add a border to your spreadsheet. The Help Menu can be a valuable tool when using a spreadsheet program. It is worth your time to become familiar with using the Help option since the Excel user manual is very abbreviated. Lotus does not even include a manual with its program when it is packaged on CD-Rom.

The Toolbar

The toolbar is located directly below the menu bar on the Excel screen. It displays a series of buttons with pictures or icons that represent short-cuts. These buttons provide a quick way to carry out certain commands that are used frequently in Excel without wading through menus and dialog boxes. The exact buttons and their order may be different on different computers. This is because the Excel program can be customized to meet your particular needs. To add, delete, or rearrange buttons choose **V**iew **T**oolbars from the menus.

To learn what function each button performs, simply move the mouse pointer over the button. Almost immediately a box will appear directly under the mouse pointer that lists the button's function. Also, at the bottom of the Excel screen, a more detailed description of the button's function will appear.

The Formula Bar

The formula bar has three separate sections. The left part of the formula bar is called the reference area since it indicates the name of the active cell. The center section remains blank until you begin to type an entry into a cell. As soon as the first keystroke is made, three symbols appear in this section. By clicking on the first symbol, an "X," you cancel the entry you were going to put into the cell. Clicking on the second symbol, a check mark, enters what you have typed into the cell. This is an alternative to using the Enter key or an Arrow key to enter the data into the spreadsheet. The third symbol, a function key, allows you to add a function to the cell entry by accessing the Function Wizard. The right part of the formula bar displays the contents of the selected cell. If the cell contains a formula, the formula bar displays the formula, and the cell itself in the worksheet displays the result of that formula.

The Worksheet Area

	A	B	C	D	E	F	G	H	I	
1										
2										
3										
4										

The worksheet area of the spreadsheet is where data is entered. The worksheet is a grid or matrix of cells that is 256 columns wide by 16,384 rows long. Each of these many cells can contain text, numbers, formulas, or graphics. Each cell has its own name or address that consists of the column letter followed by the row number. The column letters (A, B, C,..., IV) are listed at the top of each column, and row numbers (1, 2, 3, ..., 16,384) are listed to the left of each row. Therefore, the cell in the upper left corner of the worksheet is referred to as cell A1, the cell immediately below A1 is referred to as cell A2, the cell to the right of A1 is cell B1, and so on. All spreadsheets use this same cell naming technique. The active cell (the one into which any input will be placed) can be identified by a solid black border around the cell which emphasizes that cell and makes it stand out from the others.

Sheet Tabs

| | | Sheet1 / Sheet2 / Sheet3 / Sheet4 / Sheet5 / Sheet6 / | | |

Excel worksheets are stored in a format which combines multiple worksheets into one file known as a workbook. This new way of saving worksheets began with version 5.0 and has carried over to version 7.0. The new format allows several related worksheets to be contained in one file. Also, any charts that have been derived from a worksheet will be saved in that workbook or file. The sheet tabs, near the bottom of the screen, allow you to switch between worksheets and charts in a workbook. You may rename, copy, or delete any existing worksheet or chart or insert a new sheet or chart by clicking a sheet tab with your right mouse button and making a choice from the resulting menu.

Renaming a worksheet or chart can be very handy. Rather than calling a worksheet simply "Sheet 1" it may be better to call it something more descriptive such as "Budget" or "1stMonth." To rename a sheet double click on the sheet tab and type the new title.

The right- and left-pointing arrow buttons to the left of the sheet tabs are the sheet tab control buttons, which allow you to scroll through the list of sheet tabs either one at a time in either direction, or by going to the first sheet or the last sheet with just one click.

The Status Bar

| Ready | | Sum=0 | | | | |

The status bar is located directly below the sheet tabs. It contains various pieces of information such as the current state of Excel, as well as some messages. For example, most of the time the message visible on the left end of the status bar is "Ready" indicating that Excel is waiting for input. But as soon as you begin to type data, the status bar lists "Enter" as your current message, replacing "Ready." As you scroll through the menus with the arrow keys, Excel will display a short message on the status bar describing the selected menu command. Also, as you will recall from earlier, if you point the mouse at a toolbar short-cut button, the status line will display a brief description of that button's function.

NAVIGATING THE WORKSHEET

Moving around an Excel spreadsheet can be accomplished in several ways, depending on the distance to be covered. If the active cell is located fairly close to your destination cell, use the arrow keys to move to the new cell. To use the arrow keys, simply press the appropriate key once for each cell that you wish to move across. For example, assuming that the current cell is A1 and you wish to move to cell A4, press the down arrow key three times. To move from A4 to E4 press the right arrow key four times.

> **Lotus Tip**
> In the Lotus program, pressing the "Home" key makes cell A1 the active cell. For example, if the active cell is H37 and you press the "Home" key one time, the cursor will move back to cell A1 in the spreadsheet.

On the other hand, moving to a more distant cell is usually easier with the mouse. When the mouse pointer is over the worksheet area, it will be in the shape of an outlined white cross. If the destination cell is visible on the screen, place the mouse pointer over that cell and click one time on the left mouse button to make it the new active cell. To move to a cell which is not currently displayed on the screen, click on the scroll bars until the cell is visible and then click on it.

For example, if the active cell is A1 and you wish to make A40 the active cell, merely click on the arrow at the bottom of the scroll bar on the right-hand part of the screen until A40 is visible. Move the mouse pointer over cell A40 and click with the left button. Each click on the scroll bar moves the worksheet up or down one page. The box in the scroll bar moves up and down to indicate your position in the worksheet. If you wish to move up, click above the box. If down, click beneath the box. To move more quickly, you can drag the box to the desired position, and Excel will let you know your location with a message on the left side of the formula bar.

If you know the name of the cell to which you wish to move (such as A40 in the example above) use the Goto command. The Goto command will change the active cell to whichever cell you indicate. To use this command, choose **E**dit **G**oto from the menu then type in the cell address to which you wish to move and press Enter. Cell A40 should now be visible on the screen and outlined. A short-cut method of accomplishing the same task is to press the function key **F5** and simply type in the destination cell address and press Enter.

Another way of moving around the worksheet is to use the Page Up (PgUp) and Page Down (PgDn) keys. These keys shift the viewable area up or down one screen at a time. The amount of change depends on the size of the computer screen. A notebook computer may only change by twenty rows each time PgUp or PgDn is pressed, but a full size monitor will display more rows and, therefore, shift up and down in larger increments. No matter what size screen you are working with, the pointer maintains its relative position on the screen. For example, if cell A1 is the active cell and you press PgDn, your row number will change, but the pointer will still be located in the A column.

ENTERING TEXT AND NUMBERS

To enter data into a cell, begin by choosing the cell you wish to use. Place the mouse pointer over the cell and press the left button once. This makes the cell the active or current cell, which means it will be the cell into which the data you type is entered. Type the data you wish to enter. Notice that as you type, the data appears in the cell itself and also on the formula bar. If you make a mistake while you are typing, use the backspace key or the delete key to remove the unwanted characters. When you are done typing, the data can be entered into the spreadsheet by pressing the Enter key.

Another way of entering the data is by pressing an arrow key instead of the Enter key. This can save time and keystrokes if you know into which cell your next entry will be placed. Suppose you are entering a long list of numbers into column A. After entering the first number in cell A1, rather than pressing the Enter key and then the down arrow key, simply press the down arrow key at the end of the entry and it will save you a keystroke. In this way, the number will be entered into cell A1 and the active cell will immediately shift to cell A2.

Data can be entered into a spreadsheet as labels, values, formulas, or functions. It is important to understand the different types of data, because labels can not be used in numerical calculations. A label can be one or more words or some combination of letters, symbols, or numbers. A label will be automatically aligned on the left side of the cell. Remember it is information that can not be included in calculations by the program. Examples of numbers that would be used as labels but would not be included in calculations are social security numbers, dates and phone numbers.

Values are numbers that are intended to have arithmetic operations performed on them. Values are automatically aligned starting at the right border of the cell and working back to the left, as if from an imaginary decimal point at the right cell boundary.

Correcting Errors

If you realize you have made an error in a cell after the data has been entered, there are ways to correct the entry. One way to correct the data is to return to the cell and simply retype the data. As you begin typing, the old entry is erased and the new information is entered into the cell.

If the entry in a cell is long, it would be tedious to retype the whole thing if you have only made a minor error. In this case, a better way to correct an entry is to use the Excel "Edit" key, which is the function key **F2**. To use this key, click on the cell you wish to correct to make it the active cell, then press **F2**. A flashing cursor will appear at the end of the entry in the cell itself, not in the formula bar. Use the arrow keys to move through the entry, then use the backspace or delete key to erase the error and type the correct characters. When you are finished, press Enter. *Pressing an arrow key to enter the data will not work when you are using the Edit mode of Excel.*

The Undo Command

Up to this point we have discussed how to correct a cell entry. Suppose, however, that you have accidentally deleted part of a spreadsheet, or some other action that is fairly major, but unintentional. What can you do? It would be tedious to type everything that you have deleted back into the spreadsheet, so instead use the Undo command available in Excel. Each time you choose Undo, the program backs up, to undo the last action requested.

Provided you have enough memory space, the program is capable of retracing up to 99 steps for you. This can be a life saver if you

| **Lotus Tip** |
| In Lotus, the Undo command will only undo one step. Undo will not retrace multiple steps as it does in the Excel program. |

realize you have done something to your spreadsheet that you didn't mean to do. There are two ways to access the Undo command. Choose **E**dit **U**ndo from the menus or click on the Undo icon located on the toolbar. The Undo icon is the button with a left-pointing arrow on it. Each time you choose this command from the menus or click on the icon on the toolbar, the program will undo one action.

Adjusting Column Width and Row Height

If the label or text you are entering into a cell is too wide for that cell, several things can happen. Suppose you wish to enter the text "My Monthly Budget" into a cell as a heading. That phrase is longer than the default column width in the spreadsheet, so the text will run over into the next cell. As long as the next cell is empty, Excel allows the text to run over and does not truncate it. But if there is a data entry of any kind in the next cell, the program will cut the new text from view. The full text is still entered into the cell, and it will appear in its entirety in the formula bar, but it will not be visible totally in the cell, since it will be truncated because of the next entry.

| **Lotus Tip** |
| The Lotus program also notifies you that the number does not fit in the column, but rather than pound signs, it displays a series of asterisks at the top of the cell. The number will only appear in the cell if you adjust the column width to accommodate it. |

It is usually obvious when text is truncated, but truncating numbers could lead to confusion. To avoid this problem, when the column is too narrow to display a number Excel converts the number to a series of pound signs (######). This is your cue to adjust the column width.

If you want the text or value to be contained totally in one cell, the column width can be adjusted to allow this. There are several ways to adjust the column width in Excel. One way to accomplish this is to click on the column letter heading to highlight the entire column. Then choose F**o**rmat (note that

> **Lotus Tip**
> In Lotus, the equivalent menu command for Excel's "F**o**rmat" is "**S**tyle." For example, to adjust the column width in Lotus, choose **S**tyle **C**olumn Width from the menus.

you must use the "o" rather than the "F" in this case if you are using the "Alt" key rather than the mouse, since "F" is used for the "File" menu option) **C**olumn **W**idth from the menus and type in the exact number of spaces you wish the column width to be. To use this method, simply make an educated guess as to how wide the column should be to accommodate the entry.

An easier way to adjust the column width is to place the mouse pointer over the right boundary of the column heading you wish to adjust. The pointer will become a black cross when you are directly over the column boundary. Hold the left mouse button down and drag the column boundary to the width you wish it to be, either narrower or wider. Release the mouse button when the width is correct. For example, if you want to widen column C in this manner, place the mouse pointer over the boundary between the column C and column D headings until you have a black cross showing. Then hold down the left mouse button and drag the column boundary to the right until you have the width you desire. To narrow the column simply drag the mouse pointer to the left. Notice that as you are dragging the mouse, the reference area of the formula bar displays the exact width of the column as you change it.

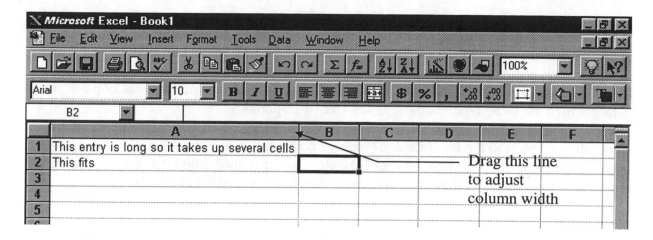

Excel also allows you to adjust a column's width according to the longest entry in that column. Suppose you wish to do this to column A. Type your entries into the column, then place the mouse pointer over the boundary between the column A and the column B headings until you have a black cross. Then double click the left mouse button. The program will adjust the column width to the length of the longest entry in that column. If longer entries are added in this column after this adjustment has been made, it must be redone.

The row height can be adjusted in a spreadsheet in the same ways the column width can be adjusted. Follow the same steps involved in column width adjustment, but instead of using the column letter headings, use the row number headings at the left to make the adjustments.

Formatting Cells

You can change the look of your spreadsheet by changing the format of the cells. Excel lets you adjust the size the look of text, the alignment of text and numbers and even the color of the spreadsheet.

Fonts

Once you have entered labels or values into a spreadsheet, any number of changes can be made in the appearance of those entries if you don't like the way they look. Excel has many formatting and alignment options available. Formatting refers to the appearance of the data. A "typeface" is a particular style of drawing letters and numbers. Excel has many styles available for use in its spreadsheets such as Times New Roman, Arial, and Courier. The typeface you choose is simply a matter of personal taste. Typeface also refers to whether the text is drawn **bold**, *italics*, or perhaps ***bold italics***.

The term "type size" refers to the size of the typeface. When typewriters were commonly used, type size was defined in characters per inch (CPI). This convention was somewhat confusing because the larger the CPI number, the smaller was the text. Today, with computers we normally refer to the type size in "points." Each point represents an increment of 1/72nd of an inch, so there are 72 points to the inch. A typeface printed at a 12 point size is larger than the same typeface printed at a size of 10 points.

Generally, we refer to the typeface and type size combination as a font. So when we say "change the font to 12 point bold Times New Roman," it is understood that we are referring to a particular typeface (Times New Roman, bolded) and type size (12 point).

Alignment

The alignment of the data means the data's position within the cell and is also part of the format. Remember that Excel, by default, displays text at the left side of a cell and numbers at the right side of a cell. Sometimes this is not the most attractive way to display the data in a worksheet. We can easily change the way that these entries are displayed through the use of alignment options. Excel provides three different horizontal alignments within a cell. We can have the text or numbers aligned with the left or right sides of the cell or centered within the cell boundaries.

Excel also allows centering of text across more than one column of cells. To accomplish this, type the text into the leftmost cell that will be used. Then highlight from that cell to the right to include all the columns across which

> **Lotus Tip**
> To center text across columns in Lotus, type the text into the leftmost cell, highlight the range you want the text to occupy, then choose Style Alignment Center Across columns. In this way, Lotus will allow you to center across columns, just as Excel does.

you wish the text to be centered. Click on the icon that looks like an "a" with arrows on each side. The text will then be centered across the columns you have chosen. If, instead, you choose the regular centering icon, the text will simply be centered within one cell.

Formatting numbers

Just as labels can be changed, the appearance of the numbers in your spreadsheet can be changed also. Numbers can be displayed in any typeface and point size you wish to use. To change the appearance of a number, click on that cell to make it the active cell, then click on whatever typeface and point size you want from the toolbar.

In addition to font changes, the appearance of numbers can also be altered by adding commas and dollar signs and by changing the number of decimal places displayed. To make these changes, begin by making the cell you want to change the active cell. From the menus choose Format Cells and then Numbers from the selections available. Choose the category desired from the box on the left side of the dialog box. Depending on what category you choose, other options will be available. If you choose "Number," you can set the number of decimal places displayed and whether commas will appear or not. You can also choose how negative numbers will appear in your spreadsheet. Negative numbers can be displayed in a different color type, using the negative sign, or using parentheses. If you select the category "Currency," you can also choose whether to have dollar signs or not.

Using Ranges

When working with spreadsheets, you may want to perform an operation on an area of the sheet that encompasses more than just one cell. Any rectangular grouping of cells is called a range. Think of a range as being just an area of the spreadsheet. A range can be one row extending across many columns, one column running down several rows, or a block that covers many rows and many columns. A range is defined by listing the two cells that are diagonally opposite from each other and placing a colon (:) between them, such as the range A1:H8.

> **Lotus Tip**
> In Lotus, a range is defined by listing the two cells that are diagonally opposite from each other and placing two periods between them, such as the range A1..H8.

Selecting a Range

Suppose you wish to make a particular change to a large number of cells in your spreadsheet. It would be tedious to change one cell at a time, especially over a large area of the sheet. Instead it would be more practical to simultaneously select the whole range and perform the changes all at once. To select or highlight a contiguous range, place the mouse pointer over a corner cell in the range, press the left button and drag the mouse in whichever direction will encompass the entire range you need, then release the mouse button. As you drag the mouse, notice the reference area of the formula bar. Excel shows you the dimensions of the range being selected.

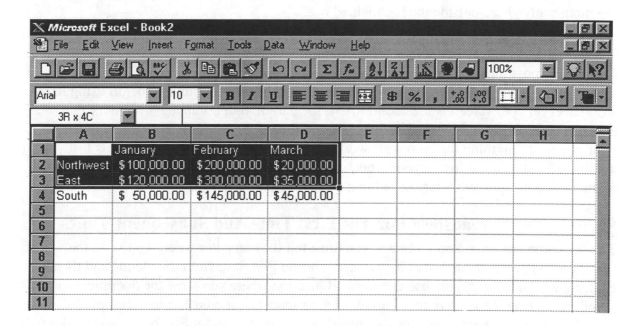

You can also use the keyboard to select a range. First change the active cell to a corner cell of the range to be selected, press and hold down the Shift key, and use the arrow keys to move in whatever directions will highlight the entire range. Note that if you release the Shift key while pressing an arrow key you will lose the highlighting.

Selecting Non-contiguous Ranges

At times you may also need to select a non-contiguous range (two or more unconnected ranges) of cells. To do this, simply select the first range as you normally would, and then hold down the Control key as you select the other ranges that you need.

C1		February	
A	**B**	**C**	**D**
1		January	February	March
2 Northwest	$100,000.00	$200,000.00	$20,000.00
3 East	$120,000.00	$300,000.00	$35,000.00
4 South	$ 50,000.00	$145,000.00	$45,000.00
5			

Hold the control key down while selecting this column

It is very important that you be allowed to select cells in Excel since, like most other Windows applications, Excel works in the "select, then act" mode. In Excel, you first select the cells that you wish to act on, then choose the operation that you want to perform. This would seem to be a minor point, but it is actually quite important. In the "select, then act" method, the cells stay selected after the operation has been performed, thereby allowing another operation on those cells without re-selecting them. For example, if you decide to change the font and the alignment of a range of cells, you need only highlight that range once. As long as the range remains highlighted, you can continue performing operations on those cells until you are satisfied with their appearance. To turn off the highlighting, simply click the mouse anywhere outside the highlighted range.

SAVING YOUR SPREADSHEET

One of the most important things to remember about working with personal computers is to save your work . . . **OFTEN**. When you load a spreadsheet program and begin using it, the worksheet on your screen is located in RAM, the part of your computer's memory that depends on a constant flow of electricity to continue. If the power is accidentally shut off to your machine, anything that you were working on that was not saved onto disk is lost. So to avoid the frustration of losing your work, save frequently. Saving a document takes only a moment and can prevent hours of redoing work that you have lost.

Saving Your Spreadsheet For The First Time And Subsequent Times

The first time you save a spreadsheet, you must tell the computer where you want the work saved and what you want to call it. To save, choose **F**ile **S**ave from the menus and then, by clicking with the mouse, choose the physical location where you want the document to be saved, such as in the C drive (hard drive) of your machine or on a 3 ½ inch floppy disk. Then type the name you want to use for the spreadsheet into the box for File Name and click on the Save button in the dialog box. At this point, a message will appear in the status bar of your screen saying that the program is saving your spreadsheet under the name you have chosen to call it. When the computer is finished saving the document, this message disappears and you are ready to continue to work on the spreadsheet.

When additions or changes have been made to the spreadsheet, it should be saved again so that these changes will not be lost if there is a power failure. Once you have done the initial save, subsequent saves are easy. Simply choose **F**ile **S**ave from the menus again, but this time the computer will skip directly to the save process and bypass asking you where to put the document and what to call it. The program assumes you want the work saved in the same location and under the same name as before. This is called a "Quick Save" and it takes only a matter of seconds to save the work you have done since the last save process was executed. This is time well spent.

You can also execute the Save command by clicking with the mouse on the Save button on the toolbar. Remember, the icons on the toolbar represent short-cut methods of executing commands. The Save icon is a picture of a floppy disk. If you have not saved the worksheet yet, clicking on this icon will lead you to the dialog box that

> **Lotus Tip**
> The Save icon in Lotus is a picture of an open file folder with an arrow pointing downward into the folder.

allows you to choose the location and name for the document. If you have done the initial save already, clicking on the icon executes a Quick Save. The same results can be accomplished by either using the menus or the icon.

Saving In Another Location Or Under A Different Name

Another feature offered by Excel with regard to saving your spreadsheet is the "Save As" option. Suppose you have saved a worksheet, then decide that you also wish to save it in another physical location in your computer or you want to save it again but under a different name. If you click on **F**ile **S**ave again, the computer will execute a quick save, simply saving the document again in the same location and under the same name. Instead, click on **F**ile Save **A**s from the menus. The dialog box will appear that again allows you to choose where you want the document saved and what you want to call it. You can change the location, the name, or both. From this point forward, however, if you execute a quick save, the document will be saved in this new location or under the new name, whatever you have changed. If you also want it saved again in the old location or under the old name, you must execute another File Save As and save it there too.

USING EXCEL FORMULAS

The real benefit of a spreadsheet program is its ability to use formulas to calculate data. A formula expresses relationships among values in a worksheet. Formulas are based on cell addresses in the spreadsheet. For example, to add two cells together, we simply tell the program to take the contents of one cell and add that to the contents of the second cell. The formula for accomplishing this task is entered into the cell in which we want the answer to appear.

Entering Excel Formulas

In Excel, all formulas begin with the equals sign (=) to indicate to the program that a formula will follow. Without the equals sign, the program will treat the formula as text and will not calculate a result. The operators +, -, *, /, and ^ mean add, subtract, multiply, divide, and exponent respectively when used in a formula. For example, typing the formula =A1+A2 into cell A3 tells the program to add the contents of cell A1 to the contents of cell A2 and display the sum in cell A3.

Remember, the cell A3 will contain the answer, but the formula bar will contain the formula. The contents of cells A1 and A2 must be either values, formulas, or functions. The cells may also be blank, which would be treated like zeros.

Arial			10		B	I	U		
A3			=A1+A2						

	A	B	C	D	E
1	123				
2	456				
3	579				
4					

Another way to enter a formula into a cell is to use the pointer method. This involves using the mouse to point to cells that we want in the formula. To add the contents of cells A1 and A2 using the pointer method, start by clicking on cell A3, where the formula is to be inserted. Then type the equals sign, point at A1 and click, type the plus sign, point at A2 and click, then hit Enter. Notice as you did this, the formula bar displayed each cell and sign as you worked. This method will give you the same result as typing the formula directly into the cell. It is an easier method to use if one or more of the cells you want included in your formula are outside the viewable area of your spreadsheet. In this case, to enter the formula directly into the cell, you would have to know the cell addresses you are including. With the pointer method, you can start your formula at a cell you know, then move the mouse to the other cells that may be off your screen.

Using Parentheses To Control Order Of Operations

Using the mathematical operators +, -, *, /, and ^ seems fairly straightforward, but in some cases it is more complicated than it appears. For example, let's say we want Excel to evaluate the following equation:

$$X = 3 + 4 / 2$$

If Excel simply worked through the equation from left to right, the answer would be 3.5. But Excel does not work that way. Excel evaluates equations using a procedure called operator precedence, which means that certain mathematical operators take precedence over others. Normally, exponents are calculated first. Multiplication and division are usually performed next, but they are equal in precedence so these operations will be performed from left to right in the equation. Finally addition and subtraction, which are also equal in precedence, are performed.

Keeping in mind that Excel works in this manner, look at the equation again. The division would be performed first, then the addition. So the answer, according to Excel, would be 5, very different from the answer we would assume if the program simply worked from left to right in the equation. But suppose for our purposes the equation will only be correct if the addition is performed first, then the division. To force Excel to perform the operations in the order we prefer, we can add parentheses to our equation, thus modifying the order of precedence. Operations that are enclosed in parentheses are always evaluated first. Modified, our equation would look like this:

$$X = (3 + 4) / 2$$

The parentheses force Excel to perform the addition first, then the division. In this way, we can be sure that we achieve the results that are valid in our situation. If you are in doubt use parentheses.

Using Built-in Excel Functions In Formulas

The Excel program has functions built into it that can be used in formulas. Functions are certain words such as SUM and AVERAGE that can be typed into formulas, telling the program to perform those tasks, without having to describe how to do those tasks to the computer. For example, by typing in the word AVERAGE, the program understands that it should add the contents of all the cells involved, then divide that total by the number of entries. The user does not have to explain to the computer what an average is since it is a built-in function of the program. These functions make it easier to build complex equations. Functions also cut down on the amount of information that must be keyed in, reducing the likelihood of errors. To use a function, choose the term that describes what task is to be performed and supply the proper cell addresses to be included. For example, to add cells A1, A2, A3, A4, and A5 and put the total in cell A6 we could just use plus signs, but that would be a fairly tedious equation to type into the cell, and an error-prone way of accomplishing this task.

$$= A1 + A2 + A3 + A4 + A5$$

Instead, by using a built-in Excel function, we can simplify the equation and minimize the amount of information that must be keyed into the cell. The same equation, using a function, would look like this:

= SUM (A1 : A5)

> **Lotus Tip**
>
> Lotus also has built in functions, but they are called @Functions, since the "@" symbol must precede the function word. Remember also that in Lotus, two periods separate the cells defining a range. For example, to add the contents of cells A1 through A8, the formula in Lotus would be
>
> =@SUM(A1..A8)

The equation must still begin with the equals sign, to tell Excel it will be calculating something, then the function SUM, then within parentheses the range of cells to be included. The true value of this method of writing a formula becomes apparent when large strings of cells must be included. It is much more efficient and less error-prone to simply type in the first and last cell in the string, rather than having to include each individual cell address in the equation.

You can also accomplish this same task by typing part of the formula and pointing with the mouse at the cell addresses to be included. To do this, click on the cell where the formula with the function is to be inserted, then type the equals sign and the word SUM followed by an opening parenthesis. Then click on the first cell in the range, type a colon, click on the last cell to complete the range and press the Enter key.

Using the Excel Function Wizard

Using functions in Excel can be very confusing. Many of the financial functions have several parameters that must be specified. To make it easier to use functions in formulas, Excel provides the Function Wizard, which is a step by step series of dialog boxes that lead you through the process of choosing the function you need and entering the necessary information. A function can be simply typed into a cell without the Function Wizard, but it is there for you if you need the assistance.

To use the Function Wizard, click on the cell into which you wish to enter the function and then type the equals sign. Click on the function button (f_x) in the formula bar. At this point, step one of the Function Wizard will appear as a dialog box on your screen. Choose the category of function you wish to enter, such as financial, statistical, etc. An alphabetical list of the functions available under that category will appear. As you scroll through the functions available, a short description of each of the functions will appear in the dialog box. Choose the function you need, then click on the "Next" button at the

> **Lotus Tip**
>
> Using functions can also be confusing in Lotus, but the program does provide helpful ways to deal with functions. By typing the equals sign, then the "@" symbol and then pressing the F3 function key, a dialog box will appear that lists the functions available in Lotus. Choose the one you want and it will appear in your cell along with the parameters required to fulfill the function. Another option when using functions is to type the equals sign into your cell, then click on the "@" symbol on the formula bar. At this point a dialog box will appear that allows you to choose from a few common functions or choose "List All." Choose the function you want and it will appear in your cell.

bottom of the dialog box. The second Function Wizard dialog box will appear allowing you to insert the information needed for your function. When you are done specifying the parameters needed, click on the "Finish" button at the bottom of the dialog box.

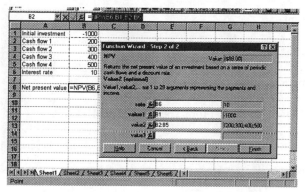

The final
result appears
here

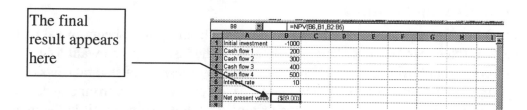

Examples of Functions

Excel has hundreds of functions built into the program, many of which are financial functions. The following is a list of the *financial* functions available in Excel 7.0. They are listed in alphabetical order in the Function Wizard under the category "Financial."

DB	Returns the depreciation of an asset for a specified period using the fixed-declining balance method.
DDB	Returns the depreciation of an asset for a specified period using the double-declining balance method or some other method you specify.
FV	Returns the future value of an investment.

IPMT	Returns the interest payment for an investment for a given period.
IRR	Returns the internal rate of return for a series of cash flows.
MIRR	Returns the internal rate of return where positive and negative cash flows are financed at different rates.
NPER	Returns the number of periods for an investment.
NPV	Returns the net present value of an investment based on a series of periodic cash flows and a discount rate.
PMT	Returns the periodic payment for an annuity.
PPMT	Returns the payment on the principal for an investment for a given period.
PV	Returns the present value of an investment.
RATE	Returns the interest rate per period of an annuity.
SLN	Returns the straight-line depreciation of an asset for one period.
SYD	Returns the sum-of-years' digits depreciation of an asset for a specified period.
VDB	Returns the depreciation of an asset for a specified or partial period using a declining balance method.

Copying and Moving Formulas

Some users feel that the copy functions are what make electronic spreadsheets so valuable. Some formulas in Excel can be rather long and detailed. The last thing you want to do is retype a formula over and over again if the same formula is necessary in several rows or columns of your spreadsheet. Luckily, Excel allows us to copy a formula from one cell to another. Copying leaves the cell contents in the original cell, but also places it in the new cell. It is equally frustrating to enter a formula into a cell and realize that it is in the wrong location. Excel also allows the contents of cells to be moved. Moving the contents of a cell involves eliminating what is in the original cell and placing the contents only in the new location.

Relative versus Absolute Cell Addressing

As a formula is copied, Excel automatically updates the cell addresses used in the formula to maintain the same relative relationships. For example, if you need to add cells A1 through A15 and want the answer in cell A16, you would type the formula =SUM(A1:A15) into cell A16. But suppose you also want to add cells B1 through B15 and put that sum in cell B16. Rather than retyping the formula into cell B16, simply copy the formula from A16 to B16. When you copy the formula, however, it will appear in cell B16 as =SUM(B1:B15).

This is called *relative cell addressing*. When the program copies the formula, it holds the same relative relationship intact. The formula requested that the contents of the fifteen cells directly above it be summed. When the formula was copied to the column next door, the intent of the formula remained the same. So the program adjusts the cell addresses and sums the fifteen cells directly above the formula, in this case in column B rather than A.

There are times when you copy a formula from one cell to another, but you don't want the cell references to change, instead you want them held constant. Excel allows cell references to be held constant by inserting dollar signs in the appropriate places in the formula. Holding the cell references constant is called *absolute cell addressing*. Suppose each time you use a formula, you need the computer to look up certain information from a table you have constructed in your spreadsheet. As you copy that formula from one row down to the next row, you don't want that cell reference to adjust down, you want it held constant so that it will continue to look up the information it needs in the table. In this case, a formula might look like this:

$$= HLOOKUP (\$D\$4 : \$E\$8)$$

The dollar signs inserted in front of the column letters and row numbers tell the program that as that formula is copied to other locations in the spreadsheet, it is not to allow the cell references to adjust. The same data is needed in each cell that uses this formula. In this example, both the columns and the rows have been held constant. It is also possible to hold just the columns constant, or just the rows, depending on what is needed in your spreadsheet.

Copying Cells and Ranges of Cells

No matter what a cell contains, the contents can be copied to other cells if necessary. For our purposes, we will look at copying formulas, but keep in mind that any type of entry in a cell can be copied to other cells, not just formulas. There are several ways to copy a formula from one cell to another. One way involves clicking on the formula cell to make it active, then choosing **E**dit **C**opy from the menus. Click on the cell you wish to copy the formula into and choose **E**dit **P**aste from the menus. The formula will be copied to the new cell, leaving it intact in the original cell.

Another way to copy a formula involves dragging with the mouse. Suppose you have typed a formula into a cell and you need the same formula copied to the ten contiguous rows beneath it. The easy way to copy this formula is to click on the formula cell to make it active, then place your mouse over the bottom right corner of the cell where a small black box is visible. If your mouse is in the correct position, a black cross will replace the normal white cross. Click and hold the left mouse button and drag the mouse across the cells you want to contain the copied

> **Lotus Tip**
> To copy the contents of a cell in Lotus, place the mouse at the bottom right corner of the cell to be copied. A white arrow will appear and to the right and below it black points will also appear. Click and hold the left mouse button and drag the mouse across the cells you want to copy the formula into, releasing the mouse button when you are finished.

formula, releasing the mouse button when you are finished. The formula will be copied to all the cells over which the mouse was dragged.

In addition to just copying one cell, Excel allows ranges of cells to be copied. To copy a whole range or area of a spreadsheet, click and drag the mouse across the range to be copied so that it becomes highlighted. Choose **E**dit **C**opy from the menus. Click on the upper left cell representing the new range and then choose **E**dit **P**aste from the menus. The information will remain in the original location and will also be copied to the new location.

Moving Cells and Ranges of Cells

Formulas can also be moved as well as copied. To move a formula, click on the formula's cell to make it active, then choose **E**dit **Cut** from the menus, click on the cell you wish to contain the formula, and choose **E**dit **P**aste from the menus. The formula will now appear only in the new cell, since it has been cut or moved from the original cell.

Whole ranges or areas of information can be moved as well as just individual cells. Click and drag with the mouse to highlight the range to be moved. Choose **E**dit **Cut** from the menus, click on the upper left corner cell of the area you wish the information moved into, and choose **E**dit **P**aste from the menus. The information will no longer exist in the old range, but will appear in the new range intact.

An alternative method to move cells is by highlighting the range to move and positioning the pointer midway beside and to the *right* of the range. With pointer so positioned, click and hold the left mouse button and drag the range to a new location. A shadow box will follow the mouse movement to show where you are moving the range.

Lotus Tip
To move the contents of a cell in Lotus, with the cell active, point at the upper cell boundary until the mouse pointer becomes a hand. Then click and drag the cell to the new location and release. The cell contents will be cut out of the original location and deposited in the new location.

CREATING EXCEL CHARTS

Spreadsheets are wonderful tools for organizing data, but they can be difficult to understand quickly by those who have not helped build them. Creating a graphic from the data in a spreadsheet can capture peoples' interest much more quickly than presenting the same information in spreadsheet form. A graphic can also better illustrate trends in the data that otherwise might be difficult to see if the spreadsheet has a large number of entries to muddle through. A graphic display of data can often be a much more pleasant way to view information.

Until recently, separate programs were needed to create graphics, since spreadsheet programs had no built-in graphic capabilities of their own. Excel is an integrated program, meaning the graphic capability we need is included in the spreadsheet program and no other program is necessary to build a chart.

> **Lotus Tip**
> Lotus is also an integrated program. Refer to the appendix for instructions on how to create charts in the Lotus program.

Using the Excel Chart Wizard

The Excel Chart Wizard is a series of dialog boxes that guide you step by step through the transformation of spreadsheet data into a graphic or chart. Each dialog box will ask for certain information to be provided so that the program can create the chart. Once the steps in the Chart Wizard are complete, the newly created chart can be formatted so that it looks exactly the way you want it to look.

Selecting The Data And Location Of The Chart

The first step in creating a chart in Excel is to select the desired data from the spreadsheet. To select the data, click and drag with the mouse to highlight the rows or columns you wish to chart. Remember if you wish to include non-contiguous ranges of the spreadsheet in your chart, highlight the first section as you normally would, then to highlight other sections press the Control key on the keyboard and highlight the information. If you do not hold down the control key while highlighting the additional data, the original data's highlighting will turn off and your information will not be selected.

Once the data has been selected, choose **I**nsert C**h**art from the menus. Another menu will appear that gives two options for creating the chart. By choosing "On this sheet" the chart will be created, saved and displayed directly on top of the spreadsheet from which the data is taken. This is called an embedded chart because the chart is embedded within the worksheet.

Once you have clicked on this option, the mouse becomes a black cross with a small chart icon attached to it. Move the mouse until it is located where you want the upper left corner of the chart to appear on the spreadsheet and click once. Your chart will now be created in this location.

By choosing the option labeled "As new sheet," the chart can be created as a separate window. By clicking on this option, the program takes you directly to the Chart Wizard.

You do not choose where to put the chart since this option will automatically create the chart as a whole new window.

Selecting The Chart Style And Titles

Once you have selected the data and chosen the location for your chart, the first dialog box from the Chart Wizard will appear on your screen. Step One in the Chart Wizard asks you if the selected data is correct. If you are satisfied that you have highlighted the correct data from your spreadsheet, click on the button labeled "Next" located at the bottom of the dialog box.

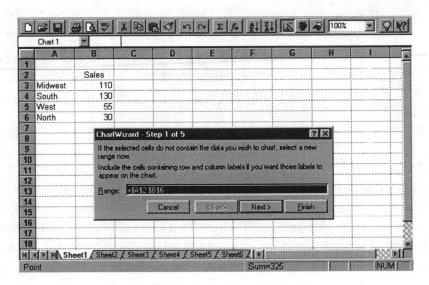

Step Two offers a choice of several different chart styles such as column, line, pie, 3-D, etc. The default chart style in Excel is the column chart. In other words, if you do not specify a chart style, the program will automatically create your chart as a column chart. Choose the style you wish to use, then click "Next" at the bottom of the dialog box.

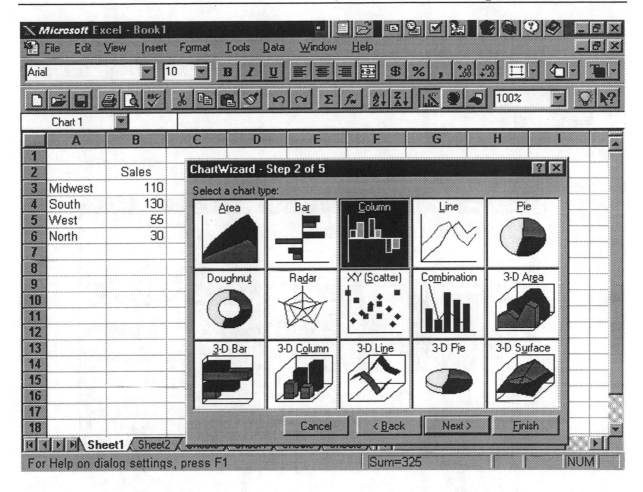

The third dialog box allows you to further define exactly what style of chart you want. For example, if you choose column as your style in Step 2, in Step 3 you will be given a choice of ten different column chart styles, some with chains connecting the columns, some with gridlines, etc. Choose the style you wish and continue by clicking "Next" again. Step 4 gives you a sample chart that shows how your chart will basically look and asks about the axis labeling. Usually Excel has defined this labeling for you correctly, so accept their default settings and move on by clicking on the "Next" button.

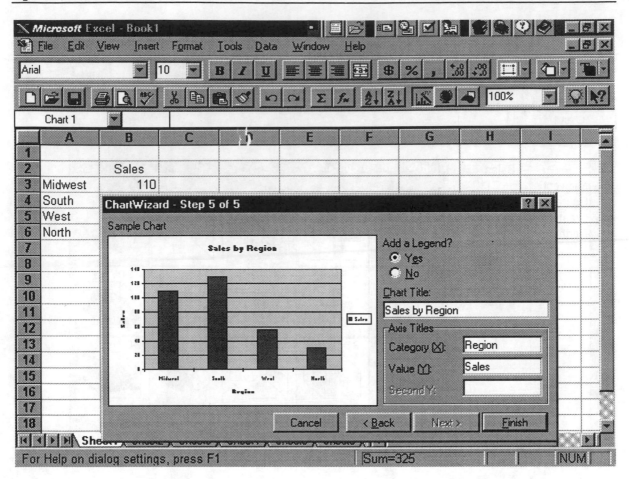

Finally, the last dialog box or Step 5 of the Chart Wizard appears on your screen with the sample chart visible. This step covers several items that will make the chart more understandable. First, a legend can be included or omitted, depending on personal preference. Also, the chart and the axes can be given titles. To add a title to the chart, move the mouse so that it is pointing at the title box, click the left button one time to place a flashing cursor in the box, and type the title you want for the chart. After typing in the title, DO NOT PRESS THE ENTER KEY. If you do, the Chart Wizard will close and you will not be able to enter axis titles at this time.

Instead of pressing Enter, once you have typed the title, press the Tab key one time to move your cursor to the X axis title box. Type the label that is appropriate for that axis. Remember the X axis is the horizontal or category axis on your chart. After typing this title, press the Tab key once again to move the cursor to the Y axis label box. The Y axis is the vertical or value axis on the chart. Type an appropriate entry for this axis. Then click the "Finish" button at the bottom of the dialog box. You have now completed the Chart Wizard. If your chart was created embedded in the spreadsheet, it will appear with the spreadsheet data in the background. If instead you chose to create the chart as a separate sheet, the spreadsheet will disappear from view and only the chart will be visible in its own new window on your screen.

If you did not add all the titles you needed to your chart while you were in the Chart Wizard (maybe you pressed ENTER after typing your chart title), all is not lost. Choose Insert Titles from the menus and then click on the appropriate boxes for the titles you want to add. Click on "OK" and you are returned to your chart. The program has now added a text area wherever you requested one in the previous step. Simply click once on the title box and type in the title you want to add. Follow the same procedure to type the axes titles if they are being added at this point also.

Suppose you have just constructed a column chart using the Chart Wizard and you realize that the chart would look better as another style of chart. With your mouse pointing anywhere in the chart, click the right button one time. A menu box will appear that allows you to select the chart type again. Select the style you want, click on "OK" and your chart will reappear on your screen as the new style rather than as a column chart.

Formatting The Chart

Once the Chart Wizard is complete, many things can be done to a chart to change its appearance. This is called formatting the chart. In Excel, each different item or element in the chart, such as the titles, the axes, or the labels, is treated as a separate "object" and can be selected and edited independently from the other items.

There are two different ways to select an item for editing. One way to edit requires that you simply point at the item with the mouse and double click the left mouse button. The Excel program is very sophisticated. It understands what item you have double clicked and knows what can be done to that item in terms of editing it. The program responds to the double click by bringing up a dialog box which presents the appropriate menus for formatting the item you have selected.

For example, if you want to change the font of the chart title, simply point the mouse at the title, double click the left button, and a dialog box will appear on the screen that is titled "Format Chart Title." This dialog box presents menus allowing you to select "Patterns,"

"Font," or "Alignment." By selecting "Font" you can change the style of lettering, point size, make it bold or italics, and several other features relating to the appearance of the lettering.

If you point at the value axis and double click the left mouse button, you can change the appearance of that axis in several ways. Besides changing the font of the numbers on the axis, you can also choose "Scale" from the menus presented and change the minimum, maximum, and major or minor units represented on that axis. This can change the look of a chart tremendously.

Another way to format a chart is to point with the mouse at the item you wish to change, click once with the left mouse button to select the item, then click once with the right mouse button. A menu box will appear that offers choices as to what you wish to do next. Among the alternatives will be a formatting choice. By clicking on that choice, the same dialog box will appear that was presented by double clicking the left mouse button as discussed earlier.

Enhancing The Chart With Arrows And Text

Up to this point, all of our formatting changes have involved changing items that were already in the chart. These items are called "attached text" because the program attaches them to the chart where it wants them to appear. The title always appears at the top of the chart. The axes titles always appear next to and below the appropriate axis. There is no choice as to where these items will be placed by the program. But Excel also allows the use of "unattached text." This is text that is placed exactly where you want it to appear.

To add unattached text to an embedded chart, double click on the chart to make it active and simply type the piece of text you wish to add. The text will appear in the formula bar as you type it. Press the Enter key and the program will automatically place that text in approximately the middle of the chart. Point at the text with the mouse, hold down the left mouse button and drag the text to where you want it placed. Release the mouse button and the text is deposited. Unattached text can be formatted, just as attached text can be. To add unattached text to a chart that is a separate window, you do not need to double click on the chart, since it is the only occupant of the window it does not need to be selected. Follow the other steps as you would for an embedded chart.

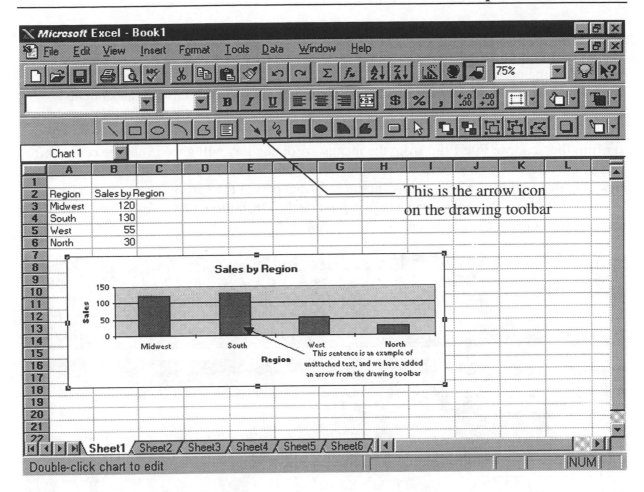

Arrows can also be added to a chart for emphasis. To add an arrow, choose **V**iew **T**oolbars from the menus and then click on the box next to the word "Drawing" in the list of available toolbars and click on "OK." This will add another toolbar to your screen that is not normally in view. Click with the left mouse button on the arrow icon, then move the mouse to the place where you want the arrow to begin (the non-pointed end). Click and hold the left mouse button and drag to form your arrow. It can be as long or short as you wish and can point in any direction on the chart. When the arrow looks the way you want it to look, release the mouse button. An arrow, combined with unattached text, can emphasize a particular value or portion of a chart that you want to make sure your audience does not miss.

PRINTING

When an Excel worksheet is displayed on the computer screen, it is a "soft copy" of the work, but sometimes you need a copy that you can take with you to a meeting or one on which you can make written notes. Printing allows you to obtain a "hard copy" of your worksheet or chart. If you are printing a small worksheet, choose **F**ile **P**rint from the menus and when the dialog box appears on the screen, click on the OK button. By default, Excel will print one copy of the entire worksheet.

Printing A Selection

There are times, however, when just a portion of a spreadsheet needs to be printed. For example, some professors keep track of students' grades by using a spreadsheet. When the grades are posted, the spreadsheet can be printed omitting the column with the students' names for privacy reasons. In this case, we would want to print only part of the spreadsheet, not the whole thing. To do this, start by highlighting the section of the spreadsheet you wish to print, then choose File Print from the menus. A dialog box will appear. In the center left part of the box will be a section titled "Print What" and the first option is "Selection." By choosing this option, the program will print only that part of the spreadsheet that you have highlighted. From this point, you can just click on the OK button, or you can first choose how many copies of the document you want printed.

Print Orientation

There are also some other choices we can make when we print a spreadsheet. Choose File Page Setup from the menus, then choose Page from the selections and a dialog box will appear that offers some alternatives as to how the spreadsheet will look when it is printed. First, you have a choice of printing in Portrait or Landscape orientation. Portrait means your spreadsheet will print normally, 8 ½ inches wide by 11 inches long. Landscape turns your spreadsheet sideways for printing so that the paper is 11 inches wide and 8 ½ inches tall. Some spreadsheets look better in one orientation rather than the other.

Fitting The Spreadsheet To A Single Page

Another option available in this dialog box is the scaling of the printout. If the spreadsheet is larger than one page, but you really want it to print all on one page, choose the "Fit to" option under Scaling. By default, Excel will fill in the number of pages as "Fit to 1 page wide by 1 page tall." The program will do everything in its power to reduce the size of the spreadsheet so that it will fit on one page for printing.

What You See Is What You Get (WYSIWYG)

If you are not confident that your spreadsheet will print the way you want, it is a good idea to view the spreadsheet before you print, just to make sure you do not waste paper printing something that does not look right. To view the spreadsheet just as it will print, choose **F**ile Print Pre**v**iew from the menus. Your spreadsheet will appear exactly as it will print. If it is too small to read, click on the "Zoom" option. Notice at this point the mouse pointer becomes an icon of a magnifying glass as you inspect your work. If you are happy with what you see, choose "Print." If you wish to make changes before you print, choose "Close" and the program returns you to the spreadsheet in normal view. An option such as Print Preview which allows you to view exactly what will print is called WYSIWYG (wiz'-ee-wig), an acronym for "What You See Is What You Get." This is available in most programs now, including spreadsheets as well as word processing programs. The purpose is to save time and paper by avoiding wasted printouts.

Printing Charts

To print a chart that has been created as a separate window, simply bring the chart up on your screen and follow the normal procedures for printing. However, if you created your chart on top of the spreadsheet and you want to print it on a separate page, begin by double clicking on the chart to put it into the edit mode. Choose **F**ile **P**rint from the menus and continue as you normally would print, selecting the orientation, number of copies, and anything else you wish to choose.

If you want to print the chart on the same page as the worksheet, select the range you wish to print, including both the spreadsheet and the chart in that range. Choose **F**ile **P**rint from the menus and continue as usual in printing your work.

OPENING EXISTING FILES

Once you have created and saved a file, you may wish to open it again sometime in the future. To open an existing file, choose **F**ile **O**pen from the menus and a dialog box will appear from which you may select the file you wish to open.

QUITTING EXCEL

There are several ways to exit the Excel program. The quickest way is to click one time with the left mouse button on the "X" at the far right side of the title bar. Another way to close the program is to double click the left mouse button on the application control button, located at the far left end of the title bar. You can also close Excel by choosing **F**ile E**x**it from the menus. Notice that if you attempt to close the Excel program without saving your work,

Excel will display a dialog box on the screen that asks if you wish to save the changes that have been made in your work.

COMPREHENSIVE EXAMPLE

To help you apply the concepts and tools discussed so far we next provide a comprehensive example using Excel to solve a finance problem. The problem is given below and a step by step solution follows. This example has been selected because it allows us to demonstrate a large number of methods that may be helpful to you in other applications.

Example: Soft drink production expansion

A firm is considering expanding its line of soft drinks as a result of capturing market share. The new production line will cost $250,000 plus $100,000 for a new building and installation. Net working capital is expected to increase by $50,000. The new line will be depreciated over its expected 7 year life using straight line depreciation. Revenues generated by the new line are expected to be $20,000 the first year and are expected to increase at a rate of $5,000 per year thereafter. Operating costs are expected to be $10,000 in the first year and are expected to increase at a rate of $1,500 per year thereafter. After 7 years the project will have a salvage value of $10,000. The firm has a cost of capital of 12% and a tax rate of 40%. What are the net initial investment and the annual cash flows associated with the project? Compute the net present value of the cash flows.

Solution:

Problems of this nature where multiple years of cash flows must be manipulated are most easily solved using a spreadsheet program. Once the first year cash flows are entered we will be able to compute the rest of the annual cash flows by using formulas and copy commands. Let us begin by computing the initial investment.

Step 1: The initial investment

The initial investment is the sum of the purchase price, installation, shipping and working capital. We will place this on the same worksheet as the annual cash flows since the total initial investment must be subtracted from the present value of the annual cash flows to prepare a net present value profile. The figures given in the problem are in rows 2-5 and the sum function is used to compute the net investment in row 6.

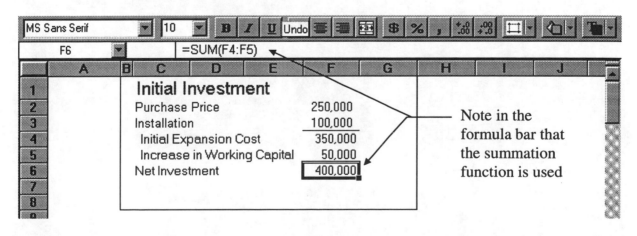

Step 2: The worksheet titles

The next step is to lay out the cash flow section of the worksheet by typing in the row and column headings. This is done below.

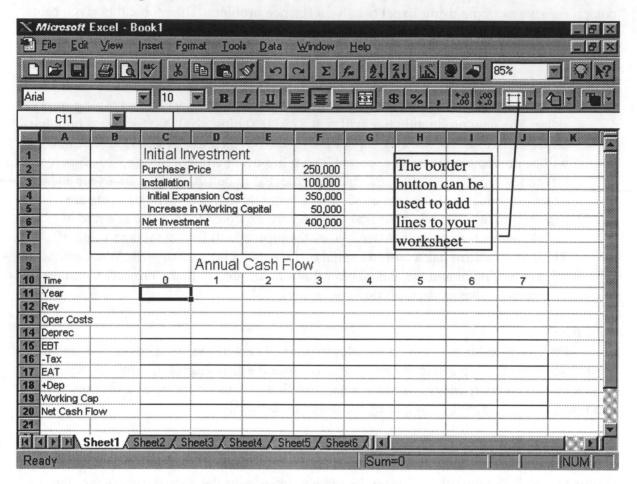

A year 0 is included to represent the present. Lines are added to the spreadsheet to make it easier to read. You could also choose to color the titles if the final version will be printed on a color printer.

Step 3: Entering the first year's cash flows

The first year's cash flows are entered into column D. Use formulas wherever possible so that most of the work will be done for you when you copy column D into the other columns. For example, earnings before tax (EBT) is highlighted so that you can see the formula. You may also choose to add $ signs and parentheses to your table to make it look more professional and easier to read.

Note that the annual depreciation is the formula ($F$6-10,000 / 7). It takes the total initial cost from cell F6, subtracts the salvage value and divides by 7 to compute the annual straight line depreciation. The dollar signs keep the reference absolute so that when the formula is copied the reference to cell F6 does not change. This way, if your estimate of the initial costs change, only one cell on the spreadsheet will have to be changed. The rest will automatically re-compute.

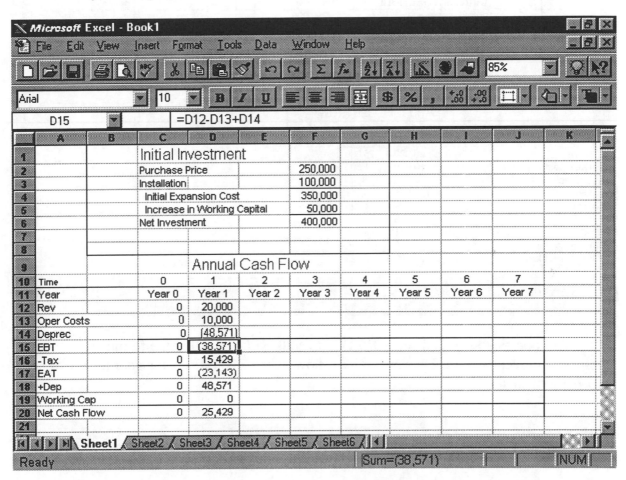

Spreadsheet Tutorial

Step 4: Year 2 formulas

In year 2, revenues are expected to rise by $5,000 and operating cost by $1,500. We will impute this information as formulas. For example, year 2 revenues will be entered as (=D12+5000). Similarly operating costs are entered as (=D13+1500). Cells 14-19 can just be copied from column D to column E.

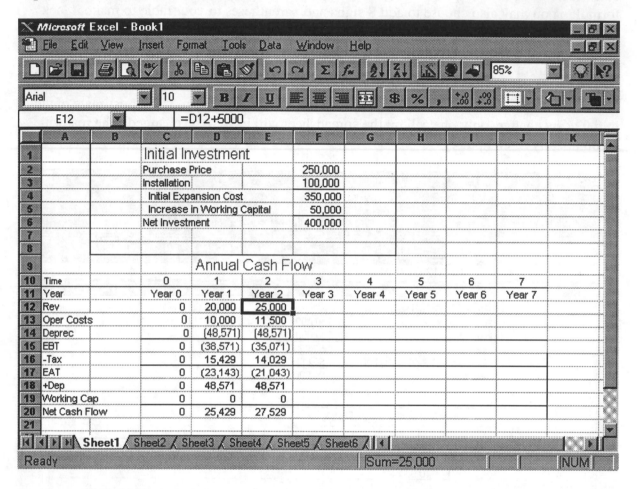

As soon as you copied cells D14-D20 to cells E14-E20, all of the formulas automatically recalculated. The new net cash flow in cell E20 reflects the additional revenues and operating costs.

Step 5: Copying to the rest of the spreadsheet

This next step is where we really see the power of electronic spreadsheets. It took a little longer to prepare year 1 and 2 cash flows than if we had just entered the figures because we wanted to use formulas. This extra effort pays off now because we can simply copy year two cash flow over into years 3-7. All of the formulas update the cells and the annual cash flows are correctly computed. We copy the year two cells by highlighting the range of cells E12-E20, and dragging the small square box at the lower right side across the columns we wish to fill. As soon as we release the mouse button the cells are updated.

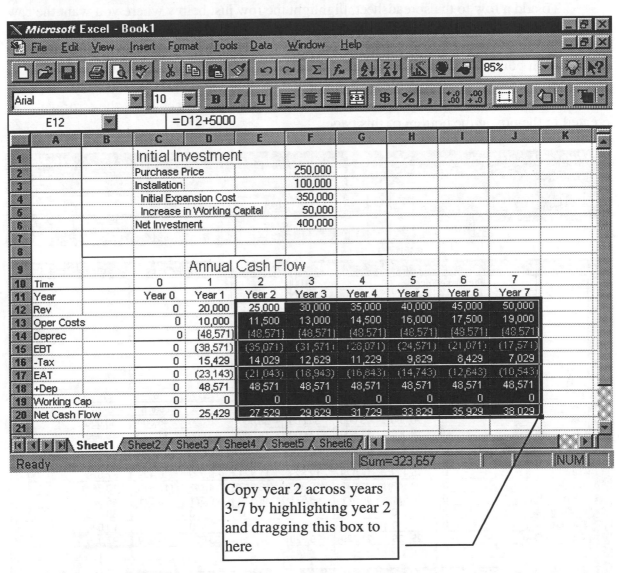

Copy year 2 across years 3-7 by highlighting year 2 and dragging this box to here

Step 6: Adding salvage and working capital

When we prepared row titles for the worksheet we remembered that in the final year we would need to account for recapturing working capital. Since this is 0 for the years 1-6, we will have to update year 7 to reflect this unique year 7 entry.

In this step we will also add a new line to the spreadsheet to allow for the salvage value of the soft drink equipment. We left this off the original template to demonstrate another powerful feature of electronic spreadsheets. If we note an error or wish to add a row or column, it is easy and quick to make adjustments.

To add a row to the spreadsheet, highlight the row just below where you want the row to be placed. If you want to add more than one row, highlight as many as you wish to add. It can be difficult to remember whether you need to highlight the row just above or just below the insertion point. Just remember that if you wanted to add a row to the very top of the spreadsheet it would be impossible to highlight above. It is a good idea to manually check a column or two to verify that the spreadsheet is working as you expect. Note the error we created in the box at the bottom of this page.

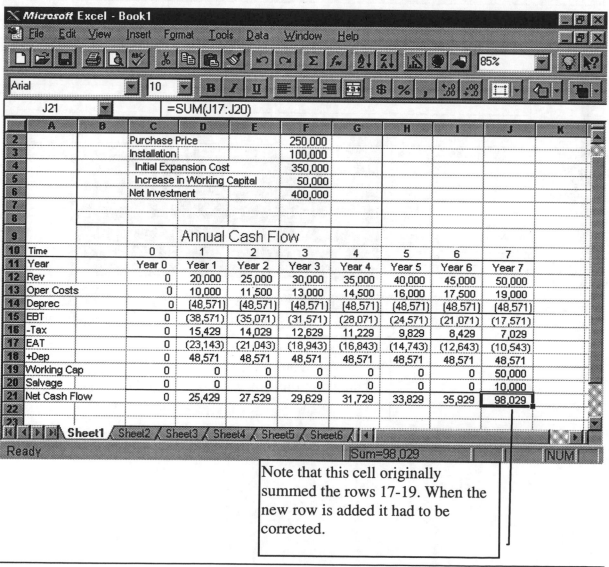

Note that this cell originally summed the rows 17-19. When the new row is added it had to be corrected.

Step 7: Computing the net present value

We are now ready to compute the net present value of the cash flows. We can find out how the present value function must be formatted by using the help button or by using the Function Wizard. The current example was prepared by choosing help index from the help menu, typing in "functions" and choosing the function index option. We then selected financial functions and PV to determine how to format the function command. This command is formatted as: PV(rate, nper, pmt, fv, type). Each of these factors is described in the help text. Rate is the discount rate (in whole number percentage), nper is the number of periods, fv is the future value, pmt is the payment if the cash flow is an annuity and type is equal to 0 if the payment is received at the end of the period, and 1 if at the beginning.

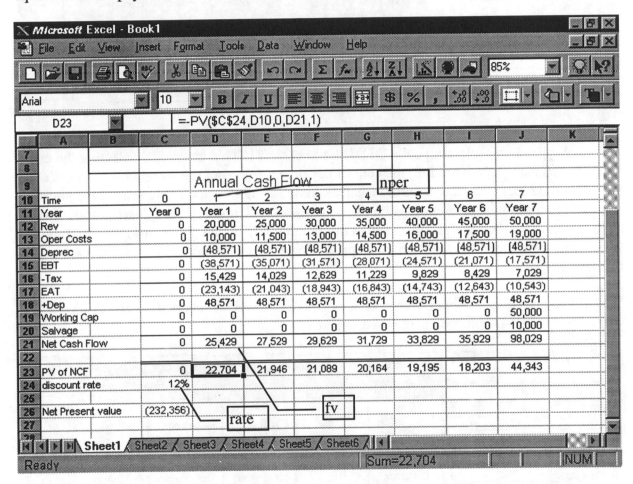

Notice how the PV function is set up with cell references so that it can be copied across the years. The reference to the discount rate was made absolute by using dollar signs ($).

Step 8: Graphing the annual cash flows

We can easily graph the annual cash flows using the Chart Wizard.

	A	B	C	D	E	F	G	H	I	J	K
10	Time		0	1	2	3	4	5	6	7	
11	Year		Year 0	Year 1	Year 2	Year 3	Year 4	Year 5	Year 6	Year 7	
12	Rev		0	20,000	25,000	30,000	35,000	40,000	45,000	50,000	
13	Oper Costs		0	10,000	11,500	13,000	14,500	16,000	17,500	19,000	
14	Deprec		0	(48,571)	(48,571)	(48,571)	(48,571)	(48,571)	(48,571)	(48,571)	
15	EBT		0	(38,571)	(35,071)	(31,571)	(28,071)	(24,571)	(21,071)	(17,571)	
16	-Tax		0								
17	EAT		0								
18	+Dep		0								
19	Working Cap		0								
20	Salvage		0								
21	Net Cash Flow		0								
22											
23	PV of NCF		0								
24	discount rate		12%								
25											
26	Net Present value		(232,356)								
27											

ChartWizard - Step 1 of 5

If the selected cells do not contain the data you wish to chart, select a new range now.

Include the cells containing row and column labels if you want those labels to appear on the chart.

Range: =$D$10:$J$10,$D$21:$J$21

[Cancel] [< Back] [Next >] [Finish]

We began by selecting cells D11-J11 and D21-J21. This is done by selecting the one range of cells and, while holding the control key down, selecting the second range of cells. Note that the chart wizard will automatically add dollar signs to the range selection signifying that this is an absolute reference. With the ranges selected choose **I**nsert **C**hart. Choose to have the chart on the current worksheet. Your pointer will change to a chart icon. Put this where you want the graph to be on your spreadsheet and press enter. The above screen will be displayed.

Choose Next if the cell reference is correct and select the chart style you desire. We will construct a 3-D column chart. Choose next.

Select Next again to choose the type of column chart you want. You will then be given the following screen to use to organize your data by rows or columns and to tell Excel if the headings are in the 1st row or column. You can play with this screen to find the options that work best for your data.

At this point you can either choose Finish and the chart will be placed on your spreadsheet or you can choose Next and have the opportunity to add a chart title and to label the axes. The following is our completed spreadsheet project.

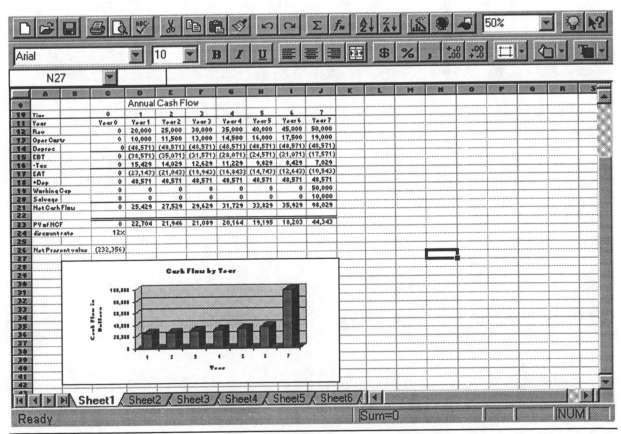

Appendix: Lotus 123

Lotus Worksheet Area

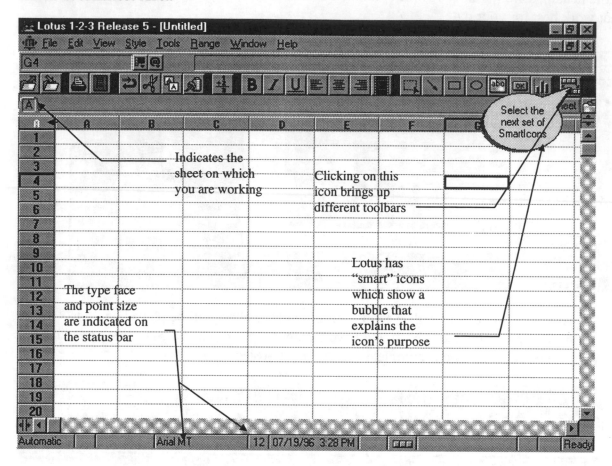

Indicates the sheet on which you are working

Clicking on this icon brings up different toolbars

Lotus has "smart" icons which show a bubble that explains the icon's purpose

The type face and point size are indicated on the status bar

Select the next set of SmartIcons

Charts in Lotus

To create a chart using Lotus 123, enter the data into a spreadsheet. Then highlight the data to be included in the chart and choose **T**ools **C**hart from the menus. At this point Lotus will look very similar to Excel. A black cross with the icon of a chart attached to it will appear on the spreadsheet. Click the mouse button where you wish the chart to appear and it will be created for you on the spreadsheet.

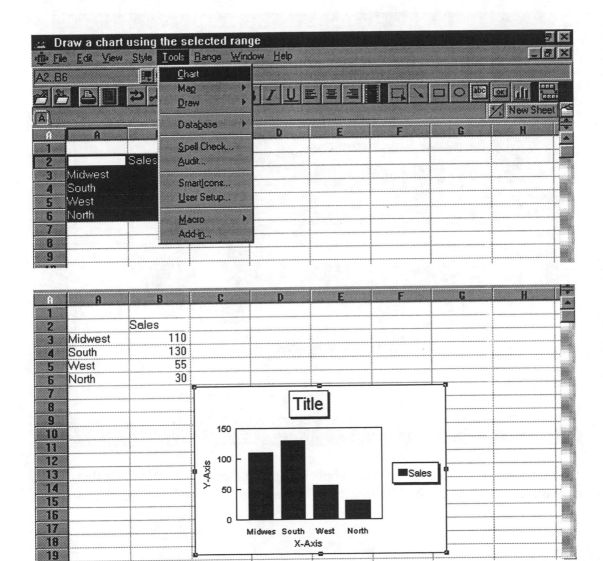

If you wish to create a chart as a separate window in Lotus, it is a little more difficult than it is in Excel. Begin by entering the data into a spreadsheet. Then click on the "New Sheet" button below the toolbar. Go back to the sheet with your data. Highlight the data as you normally would for a chart, choose **T**ools **C**hart from the menus, and then go back to the new blank sheet you created. Click the mouse button where you want the chart to appear in the new window and it will be created as a separate sheet.

Adding Titles to the Chart

Lotus creates the chart immediately on your screen with generic titles included. To edit these titles, point at the title you wish to change and double click the left mouse button. A dialog box will appear that allows you to type the title as you wish it to appear. In the example below, the main title at the top of the chart was double clicked upon and the desired title was typed into the dialog box.

You can also click on the Y axis and X axis labels to rename them. In the example that follows we have completed the chart by labeling the X axis as "Region" and the Y axis as "Sales."

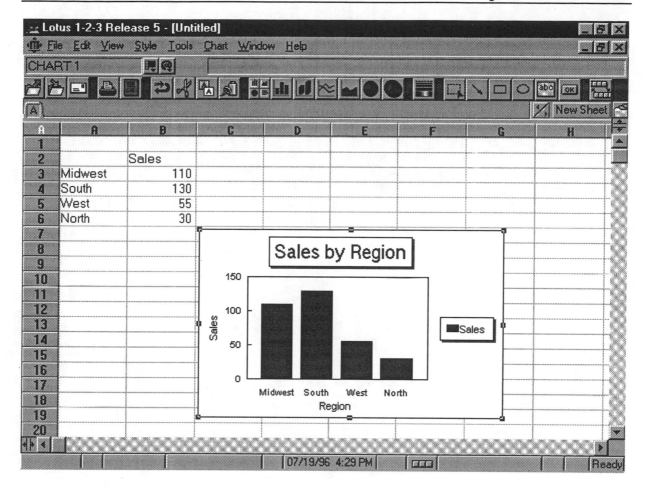

PowerPoint Tutorial

By

Debby B. Kailer

I. Beginning from the Beginning with PowerPoint

PowerPoint is a software package that will transform your presentation into an eye-catching display to keep your audience spellbound. The beauty of the software is that it is not only easy but also fun to use. This tutorial is designed to direct you through the basic steps involved in using the program and to acquaint you with its terminology. After reading the information below, hopefully you will have a better understanding of how PowerPoint can release the creative streak that lies within you.

These next few pages will teach you how to select the look you want after starting the program. A general discussion of the screen format that appears once you begin designing your presentation follows (Section II). This discussion focuses on the Main Menu positioned at the top of the screen and the toolbars that may or may not be displayed depending on how your screen is customized. Next we will examine the various types of views afforded to you as you work on your program: Slide View (Section III), Outline View (Section IV), Slide Sorter View (Section V), Note Pages View (Section VI), and Slide Show View (Section VII). Each view complements the others. Finally we will discuss printing your program (Section VIII), saving and exiting your program (Section IX), and modifying existing presentations (Section X). As you are reading, remember that this tutorial is meant to be only a basic guideline rather than an exhaustive treatment of the subject. If you find that you need additional information, there is a wide assortment of excellent books available that offer more comprehensive information. With this thought in mind, let's get started:

Starting the Program

Once you turn on your computer, you may be faced with different scenarios, depending on whether or not you are in the Windows directory. If you are greeted with the DOS prompt, "C: >" then you will need to enter the Windows directory by typing "WIN" after the **C: >**. This step is unnecessary if Windows is activated when you turn on the computer. If the program icons are automatically revealed when your computer is started, simply locate the PowerPoint icon and double-click on it. (An icon is a small, identifying picture.)

If you cannot find the PowerPoint icon it may be buried within the Microsoft Office icon. You will need to open that icon to expose the PowerPoint icon by first double-clicking on Microsoft Office icon and then double-clicking on the PowerPoint icon.

If only the Start button is evident when your computer is turned on, click on it to display the Start menu. From this menu select Programs. The Programs selection will display yet another menu listing all the programs in alphabetical order. Find Microsoft PowerPoint and click on it to open the program.

Choosing the Look That You Want

Now that you entered into the world of PowerPoint, you will have to make a decision about how to proceed. PowerPoint offers to assist you by practically developing the slides for you (you just insert the text) or it gives you the option of starting from scratch with your own ideas and color schemes. Another option falls somewhere in between: PowerPoint furnishes the templates but requires you to organize the information in the presentation. Let's look at the possibilities:

First Screen Displayed

AutoContent Wizard

This feature guides you through a process to not only format your slides, but to structure an outline for your material as well. Choose this option by selecting it (clicking on it with the left button of the mouse) and clicking the "Okay" button. To continue through the entire process, click on "Next" after you have answered the questions on each slide.

The Wizard first asks you what you want to talk about. It then prompts you to input what type of presentation you are going to give, whether it be recommending a strategy, selling a product or service, reporting progress, or communicating bad news. Once you have selected the purpose of your presentation, you must decide what form the presentation will be in (overheads, slides, etc.) and what you would like to appear on each slide (i.e. name of company, date, page number, etc.). In addition you may choose to create handout notes, speaker notes, and outline pages.

PowerPoint instructs you to select the "Finish" box so that you can see exactly what sort of outline it has developed for you. If you wish to see the presentation in Slide View, you can double-click on one of the slide icons located in front of the slide's title. (For a discussion of Slide View, see page 11). In Slide View the text color, style, and size is formatted. Of course, since you must replace the text with your own information, in essence, only the formatting and the structure of the outline are actually completed.

Template

A template is the basic design of a presentation that is carried throughout each slide. It determines how the text is formatted and what sort of background is displayed. PowerPoint supplies you with pre-existing templates that you may use if you would rather not create your own.

Once you choose the Template option and click on the "Okay" button, you will see a directory with an assortment of template names. Most of the names such as "Angles" or "Fireball" give a good indication of what sort of background will appear if that template is chosen. However, you can preview the template design by observing the box on the right once a template icon is selected (or clicked on).

After you have selected a specific template style for your presentation (by clicking on "Okay"), you must next decide which layout you will use. The layout determines where text and graphics will be positioned on each slide. Depending on the layout that you choose, space will be reserved to insert clip art (pictures), organizational charts, graphs, etc. to enhance your text or to stand alone. (For a discussion of inserting graphics, see pages 19-23.) Select the layout you desire by clicking on it and then choosing the box containing the word "Okay". A slide displaying that design and layout will subsequently appear on the screen. You must then fill in the text. Notice that you are not guided through all the options as with the AutoContent wizard because no outline is constructed for you.

Blank Presentation

If you choose this feature, everything is left up to you to decide. Choose this option by selecting it and clicking the "Okay" button. Once again, you must subsequently determine the slide layout. After the layout is selected, PowerPoint will display a screen with only the most basic text and color formatting. You will have to create your own background, font colors, etc. Obviously, this takes more work if you are novice; therefore, it's probably better to choose another option until you become a seasoned user.

Open an Existing Presentation

This is the last option available when you start up PowerPoint. If you select it and click on the "Okay" button, PowerPoint will then call up a directory of PowerPoint files. You may scroll through them until you find the one that you need. If no names are jogging your memory, then highlight one (click on it). The title page of the presentation will then appear on a small screen on the right.

Once you have located the file that you wish to open, click on that file, and then choose the "Open" box. The file that you have selected will then appear on your screen.

II. General Format of the Screen

Note: This is what your screen **may** look like if you open a blank presentation. You can customize your screen to display or to hide the various toolbars as you desire.

Program ID Bar

At the top of the screen is a bar which not only identifies the software program, but also allows you to control the screen's size.

Located on the far right side of the bar are three boxes. If the middle button displays two overlapping boxes (the "Restore Window" button), the program encompasses the entire screen. Clicking on that button will create another window so that you can open another program and run it simultaneously with PowerPoint. The button will now depict only one box instead of overlapping ones. To close the second window, click on that same button again. The overlapping boxes will reappear as the window disappears.

To minimize the window, click on the box that contains the straight line. Your program will be reduced to an icon at the bottom of the screen. You have not shut down the program, only moved it out of the way until it is needed. You may click on it at any time to return it to screen view.

To close or exit PowerPoint, click on the box that contains the "X".

Main Menu Bar

The main menu bar is found beneath the title bar. This menu allows you to perform many different options pertaining to the program on which you are working. In addition, it allows you to find, open, save and close files. This menu allows offers help if you are unsure how to proceed.

Located on the far right are three file buttons which function in a manner similar to the program buttons described above. Sometimes it is necessary to have more than one PowerPoint file open at the same time. If this is the case, these buttons enable you to minimize a file to move it out of the way, open another file simultaneously, or close a specific file.

As you browse through the Main Menu options, you can either use your pointer to select an item (by clicking on it) or you can use the "Alt" key plus the letter underlined in the item's title to select it. For example, to choose the "View" option, you would press the "Alt" key, release it, and then press the letter "V".

Once a menu item is selected you will see a box displaying a variety of choices associated with that particular item. If you choose the "File" item, for instance, choices ranging from opening a new file, to saving the file currently open, to printing the file are available. To select a command from this dropdown menu (see figure on next page), simply click on it.

Some commands in the dropdown menus have shortcuts associated with them. For example, you can access the "Save" command by pressing the Control key ("Ctrl"), holding it down, and then pressing the letter "S". (These same instructions are found in the dropdown menu.)

Sample dropdown menu

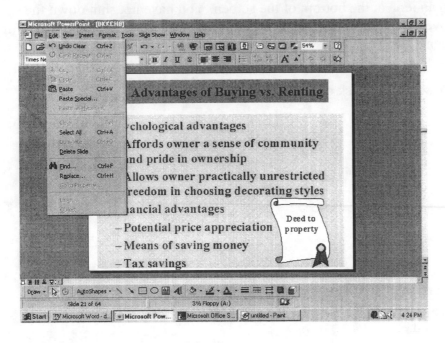

As you look at the dropdown menu, you will also notice two things:

(1) Some items listed appear to be dimmer than others.

(2) Other items listed are followed by arrowheads (▶) or ellipses (. . .).

Why are some items in lighter print than others? If an item appears in light gray or dimmer print, that item function is unavailable for use because you have not performed the prerequisites necessary to utilize that function. For example, the "Duplicate" command in the "Edit" dropdown menu is unavailable unless you have first selected something to duplicate. If you attempt to choose this command without indicating what is to be duplicated, you will receive a message stating that to enable this command you must select the object or text to be duplicated.

The items that have arrowheads or ellipses after them indicate that more information is necessary to perform that function. Once an item followed by ellipses is selected, you will be presented you with a dialog box containing yet more options. If you choose from the "Format" dropdown menu the "Font" selection, for instance, a dialog box will appear offering you choices concerning the style of font, the size, the color and so on. You must designate your choices before any changes can be applied to the slide. Items followed by arrowheads indicate that more choices (which will pop up in a box to the right of that option) are available here as well. Selecting "Alignment" from the "Format" menu will cause a box to appear with the choices of "Left," "Right", "Center", or "Justified."

Finally, as you look at some of the dropdown menus, (particularly the "View" menu) you may see that the icon beside an item may be highlighted or may have a checkmark next to it. In the case of the "View" dropdown menu, the highlighted icon indicates which view format you are currently in. Should you change the view selection, the newly selected view's icon will now be highlighted.

Again, in the "View" menu, the "Toolbar" option will reveal which toolbars are currently displayed. If there is a check beside the toolbar's title, it is displayed; if not, it is hidden. To reveal a toolbar, click on it and a check will appear. Conversely, to hide it, click on the toolbar and the check will disappear along with the toolbar.

If you have questions as you proceed which are not answered in this tutorial, the Help menu can furnish additional information. It allows you to choose a topic and then read about its application in the program. Click on the "Microsoft PowerPoint Help" selection from the Help dropdown menu. To locate a particular topic, type your question or subject heading, and select the "Search" button. Immediately, various related topics will be displayed for you to explore.

Finally, to exit from any dropdown menu without making a selection, simply click anywhere outside the menu.

Toolbars

Depending on how your screen is customized, toolbars will appear at the top or bottom of your screen. These toolbars offer you a more efficient way to perform certain tasks other than consistently accessing the Main Menu. If you plan on using PowerPoint to any extent at all, it will be to your advantage to utilize these toolbars. Don't be concerned about memorizing the function of each button. As you move the selection arrow across each button, a small title box will appear to remind you of the button's function. Let's briefly look at the main toolbars:

Standard Toolbar

This toolbar is located directly below the main menu. Here with a click of a button you are able to open, close, save, and print files; cut, copy, and paste material; undo something you just did or insert charts, graphs and clip art (pictures). (For a discussion of saving and printing files, refer to page 36. Pages 16-17 cover cutting, copying and pasting text. Refer to pages 19-23 for a discussion of clip art and pages 26-27 for a discussion of inserting graphs.) In addition, you can add a new slide or change the layout or design of the slide you are working on by using the three slide buttons. This toolbar also enables you to view your slide in black and white if you wish to focus on the text alone. You may also control how "close-up" you want to view your work with the "Zoom" button.

The Zoom control box is located on the far right side of the toolbar. If you would prefer to *zoom in* or get a closer look at your work, increase the current percentage number displayed in the box by clicking on the arrow to the right of the box. A list of alternative zoom percentages will appear beneath the one in use. Click on a number which is higher than the current one to zoom in on the screen.

Alternatively, rather than selecting a predetermined zoom percentage, you may replace the number with one of your choosing. Place the cursor after the number, press the Backspace key to delete it, and type in a larger percentage. Conversely, if you need to zoom out on your work (decrease its size), choose a smaller percentage number.

Another feature offered by the standard toolbar is the capability to add a new slide or change the slide layout of the current slide. *Creating a new slide* is accomplished by clicking on the "New Slide" button. The same layout screen that was discussed in Section I will appear asking you to designate which layout suits this particular slide. You simply select the one you want and click on the "Okay" button.

Should you wish to *change the layout of the slide* once it is created, simply click on the slide layout button, choose another format, click on the "Apply" box, and your material will automatically be rearranged. Notice that PowerPoint makes suggestions for you as to which layout you might choose based on the layout of the current slide. However, you are free to click on any layout displayed regardless of which one is already pre-selected.

The *"Apply Design" button* applies a new template to your presentation if you are not satisfied with the current choice. Upon selection of this button, you are presented with the template choices discussed in the preceding section. After previewing your choices, pick the one that you want, and click on the "Apply" button. All slides in your presentation will now display the new template style.

The Formatting Toolbar

This toolbar is located under the standard toolbar. It allows you to alter the appearance of your text. (*Note: Before any adjustments can be made to your text, you must indicate or mark which text is to be affected. This involves a procedure termed "highlighting" the text. For a discussion on how to highlight text, refer to the section on Editing Text*).

The box on the far left reveals the *font style* (in this case, Times New Roman). You can replace the one in use in much the same fashion as the procedure for changing the zoom percentage described above. Click on the arrow to the right of the style box to uncover all the styles available. Click on your preference and that style will then become the active one.

The *font size* box (in this case, "36") which is located to the right of the font style box can also be changed in the same manner. However, an even faster way to increase or decrease the font size is by using the two buttons on the toolbar containing the larger and smaller "A's". Once you have chosen the text you wish to increase or decrease in size, you can simply click on either box and that text will be enlarged or reduced in specified increments.

The next grouping of buttons allows you to modify the appearance of your text even further. Designated portions of your text may be made bolder (**B**), italicized (*I*), underlined (U), or shadowed (S).

You may also *align text* to the left, center or right with the following three buttons. The next button allows for *bulleting of your text* or removal of bullets from your text. This button toggles the bulleting feature on and off. In other words, if you highlight text that is already bulleted, clicking on this button will remove the bullets. To restore the bullets, you must click on the bullet button again.

Lastly, the two arrow buttons on the end either *promote or demote your text*. PowerPoint gives you the capability of presenting your points on five different levels according to their importance. As in any outline format, subpoints are indented under main points. Suppose you decided that one of your subpoints should instead be presented as a main point. To align that point with the other main points, you would select or highlight that subpoint and click on the "Promote" button. The text would be indented one level to the left. Conversely, if you think a main point should instead appear as a subpoint under another main point, you would indicate which text you wished to indent to the right and subsequently click on the "Demote" button.

Drawing Toolbar

PowerPoint affords you the tools to draw shapes and lines, shadow them, fill or color them with colors from its color palette or rely on the default colors. With straight lines, you may choose how thick they will be, whether they will have arrowheads, or whether they will be solid or dashed. You may insert "Word Art" if you'd like to create text with special pizzazz.

Selecting the Draw button on this toolbar reveals the Draw menu which allows you to align objects, flip or freely rotate objects, and group and ungroup them. The Draw menu also gives you the ability to order how objects will appear on the screen from the back to the front. This toolbar will be discussed in more detail in the "Drawing Objects" section of the tutorial.

The Scroll Bar

The Scroll Bar is located on the right side of the screen (see figure on next page). This bar allows for movement throughout the presentation or up and down the slide that is currently displayed on the screen. Located on the scroll bar is the scroll box – a rectangle. If you click on the scroll box, the current slide's number and title pop up.

To move quickly to another screen in your presentation, click on the scroll box, hold down the left button on the mouse, and drag the box down the bar. As the box moves, the corresponding screen number and title will appear at the left indicating where you are in your presentation. If you release the mouse button at that point, that particular screen will be displayed.

If you merely want to move to the slide preceding or following the present one displayed, click on the double arrow boxes at the very bottom of the bar. The arrows pointing upward will call up the previous slide and those pointing downward will summon the next slide.

In addition to allowing for mobility throughout the presentation, the scroll bar also enables you to move up and down the slide itself. This function won't be useful if the entire slide is already visible on the screen. However, in some cases, especially when you have zoomed in for a closer view (by changing the zoom percentage on the Standard toolbar), the entire screen won't be visible. In such a situation, the single arrows located at the top and bottom of the bar become necessary.

The View Buttons

Just above the Drawing toolbar on the lower left-hand side of the screen are the View Buttons. Each button dictates how your material is viewed on the screen as you are creating slides. To some extent, each view also limits how you may modify your presentation. We'll examine each one briefly for now.

The first button on the left, the *Slide View*, displays only one slide on the screen at a time. This is the view that is the most versatile; you will use it to rearrange text; add Clip Art, graphs, and tables; and generally modify the layout of the presentation. This is also one of the views which enables you to create new slides.

The next button is called the *Outline View*. This view displays only the text in the presentation in outline form. Because this view is limited to the text alone, it is most useful for focusing on the content of your presentation. While you may alter to some extent the text formatting in Outline View, sometimes you will not be able to see the results until you revert to Slide View. Outline View, like Slide View, also allows for the creation of new slides. However, text is the only thing that can be added to the newly created slide. If you want to add other features to embellish your presentation (like Clip Art), you must do so in Slide View.

Next to the Outline View button is the *Slide Sorter View*. In this view, each slide is miniaturized so that you are able to see the overall layout of your entire presentation. If you wish to rearrange your slides, delete a slide, or apply special effects governing how each bullet will appear during the presentation, this is the view to use. However, in this view, you cannot alter individual slides. You may insert new slides, but you cannot add any text or graphics to the newly created slide.

The *Notes Pages View*, located to the right of the Slide Sorter View button, enables you to create notes to accompany each slide. This view displays a miniaturized slide with blank space reserved below it for insertion of your own notes. These notes, which may be printed to be used in a presentation, are not seen by the audience. As with the Slide Sorter view, this view does not provide for any modification to individual slides.

Lastly, the *Slide Show View* enables you to see how your presentation will play to the audience. Your slides no longer are shown surrounded by the menus and toolbars. Instead, each slide fills the entire screen as it will when you are presenting it to the audience. When this view is active, it appears as though your presentation has taken on a life of its own. The Slide Show View mode incorporates the choices you have made concerning how bullets appear on the screen and how the slides will transition from one to the next. (These special effects are called animations and transitions. Both subjects will be discussed later.)

III. Creating Slides in Slide View

Now that we have a brief understanding of each view and its function, let's examine them individually, starting with the Slide View. Because it is the most versatile, this is the view you will probably be working with more often. PowerPoint will automatically call up Slide View after you have chosen the layout for the slide you are creating. As stated earlier, this view allows you to create text, alter text, insert graphics, and modify graphics.

Once you begin working in Slide View, you will notice that color schemes and font formats have already been established by default. For example, the title box on each page may be filled with a color you don't like or it may have no fill color at all. Perhaps the font size is too big or too small. Of course, you may change these at your discretion as you create each individual slide. However, PowerPoint provides a much more efficient way of establishing the format of your entire presentation. It's called a Slide Master.

Slide Master is a hidden slide on which you designate default characteristics (like the size and color of your text, the background color of the title box, and the page number) which you want to appear on each slide. You can override these selections on individual slides if you wish. Otherwise these features will appear on every slide throughout the presentation.

The Slide Master

How do you access Slide Master? You may select "Master" from the "View" dropdown menu. Highlighting this selection will reveal another box listing the masters available. As you can see, there are masters available for handouts and notes as well. An even quicker way to reveal the Slide Master, however, is to hold down the Shift key while you click on the Slide View button.

Slide Master Sample

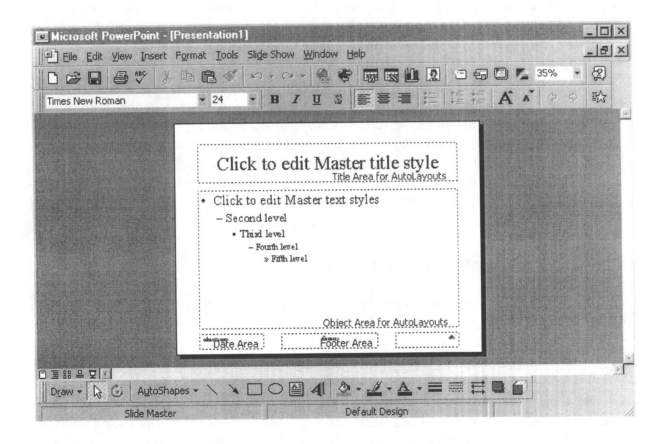

Once you've accessed Slide Master, you are free to make any changes you'd like to appear on each slide. If your preference is for a bullet shaped like an arrow instead of a diamond, you can change the bullet on the Slide Master and it will appear as an arrow on every slide.

Slide Master is also your powerful ally if you'd like to repeat any information (such as the name of your company) on every slide. Just keep in mind that whatever changes you make on Slide Master will universally affect each slide in your presentation. If you do not wish for a particular slide to, say, display the name of your company, then you must delete the name of the company on that individual slide. Consequently, you want to be sure that the choices you pick are those you want to see throughout your presentation.

Inserting and Editing Text

If you are familiar with Microsoft Word or other types of word processing software, you will already be familiar with basic procedures used to edit text. However, even if your knowledge of these word processing tools is limited, you will find the word processor in PowerPoint to be very user-friendly.

Inserting Text

PowerPoint lays out text boxes for you, depending on the type of layout you choose when you create a new slide. Some of the layouts do not contain text boxes, but odds are that you initially will choose one that does. When a text box is displayed in a slide format, you must click in the text box to begin typing. (The cursor will change to an "I-beam, indicating that you are ready to type text.) Remember that PowerPoint automatically bullets each point as you type it.

As you type, the word processor wraps the sentence onto the next line. Don't use the "Enter" key until you have completed typing that point. If you press "Enter" at the end of the line, PowerPoint will assume that you are ready to move on to the next point and a new bullet will appear. (The bullets can be turned on and off with the "Bullet" button on the Formatting toolbar.)

Let's say that you want to add two subpoints indented under a main point on your slide. After typing in the main point, press "Enter", creating another bullet positioned as a main point. To indent the text to the right, you have two options:

1) Press the Tab key and the position of the bullet will be indented to the right. Notice also that the appearance and color of the bullet may change depending on how you have formatted that level on your Slide Master. Each time you hit the "Tab" key the text will be indented further. In addition, the text will take on the font size and color designated for that particular level. You may indent (or demote) the text up to five levels.
2) Place your cursor anywhere in the line you wish to indent and click on the Demote button on the Formatting toolbar.

Now that you've finished typing in your second subpoint, you are ready to add another main point that needs to be positioned under the first main point. Instead, however, when you hit the "Enter" key after the second subpoint, PowerPoint displays a third indented bullet. In order to promote the text (or move it to the left), hold down the Shift key while pressing the "Tab" key or click on the Promote arrow on the Formatting toolbar.

Text with Subpoints

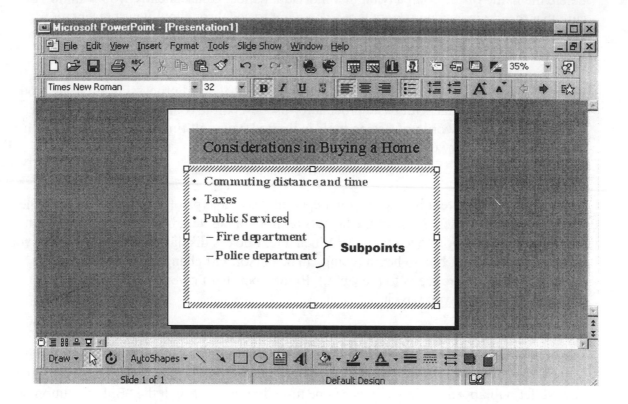

What if my text doesn't fit in the box? Change the size of the text box! You will soon see after working with PowerPoint for a very short time, that nothing is set in stone. If, for example, while typing the text in the box, you realize that it will not fit, you can expand your box to accommodate the text.

To change the size of the text box, you must first select it. (Selecting objects will be discussed in more detail later, so for our purposes here, we will keep the explanation brief). Place the arrow somewhere along the border of the box and click on the left side of the mouse. Immediately the box will be outlined in light gray with one or more handles (small boxes) on each side.

As you move the arrow across these handles, its appearance will change to a two-headed arrow. When the arrow has assumed this shape, if you click with the left button and continue holding it down, you can modify the size of the text box by dragging its side to the right or left (you'll be able to preview as you're dragging). Once the size is satisfactory, release the button and the box will be re-sized. Notice that you can widen it, make it taller, or accomplish both simultaneously by clicking on one of the diagonal handles on the corners.

If, instead of a two-headed arrow, the pointer changes to a four-cornered arrow, you will be able to drag the entire box in its original shape to another location on the screen by clicking on the left button on the mouse.

What if I want to type outside the text box provided? Even though PowerPoint offers you many options for text layout, sometimes you need to place text (usually a line or two) where there is no text box. This is especially true if you wish to label graphics incorporated into your screens. To meet this need, PowerPoint gives you the capability to create your own text box. (Remember that when there is a text box already present on the screen, you simply place your cursor within the box, click, and begin typing.)

If you wish to type outside the text box, you must rely on the Text Box button on the Drawing toolbar. Selecting that button will enable you to create your own text box by clicking and dragging. Once it is drawn, clicking inside the box will cause a cursor to appear which permits you to type text.

A word of caution, however: Creating your own text box means that PowerPoint makes no provisions for formatting it to fit the screen. You must adjust the box to make sure that it does not flow off the screen.

Editing Text
No one types everything perfectly the first time. Fortunately, editing text is a painless procedure in PowerPoint. You can cut, paste, copy, delete, move and insert text at will. Remember that when the selection arrow enters a text box, it will change to an I-beam indicating that you can perform some function associated with text. You will be unable to edit the text until the I-beam appears.

Inserting text is the most uncomplicated text function because it requires no marking or highlighting of the text. To insert text, place the cursor where you wish to add the text and click. Once the cursor is blinking steadily you can begin typing. The word processor in PowerPoint automatically inserts the text that you type by pushing the letters or words that follow your insertion point further to the right

However, if you are attempting any function besides inserting text, you must indicate which text you wish to edit by highlighting it.

Highlighting Text
To highlight follow these steps: (1) Place the cursor on either side of the text to be edited, click on the left button and drag the cursor across the text until it is completely enclosed in a black box. As the text is being highlighted, it becomes brighter so that it remains visible. (2) Release the button. (3) Once you have finished the editing, click anywhere else on the screen to remove the highlighting.

A Text Box Containing Highlighted Text

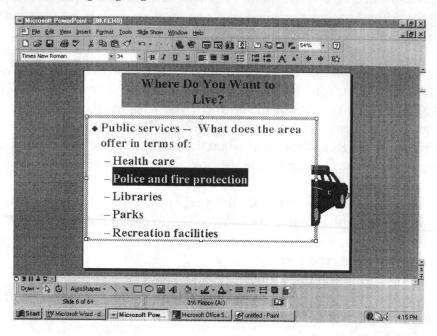

You may highlight an entire word by simply placing your cursor somewhere in that word and quickly clicking twice. Likewise, you can highlight an entire paragraph by placing your cursor somewhere within the paragraph and clicking quickly three times. If you wish to highlight a bulleted point and all the subpoints under it, place your cursor over the main bullet and click three times.

If you wish to delete text, highlight it first. At this point you can either choose the "Clear" command from the "Edit" dropdown menu or you can press the backspace key on your keyboard. If you want to replace the material that you are deleting with other text, there is no need to clear it first. All you need to do is to start typing the new text and it will automatically replace the highlighted text.

To move text, first highlight it. Then, place the selection arrow on the text and click. A small box will appear at the arrow's base that signifies that the text may be moved. While holding the left button down, drag the text to its new location and release the button. As you move the text to its new position on the screen, you will see a vertical bar jump between the words. This bar indicates where the text will be positioned if you release the button on the mouse at that point.

To cut or remove text and place it elsewhere in the presentation, highlight what you wish to cut and then either choose the "Cut" selection from the "Edit" dropdown menu or press the Control key (Ctrl) + the letter "X". The text that you have cut is now placed on a clipboard and can be recalled later if needed. (A clipboard is a temporary holding area within the computer's memory.)

To paste the "Cut" text elsewhere in the presentation, place your cursor where you would like to re-position the text. Then either choose "Paste" from the "Edit" dropdown menu or press the control key (Ctrl) + the letter "V". The text will be recalled from the clipboard and subsequently inserted where you have specified.

A word of caution concerning the clipboard: Only the most recently "cut" item will be available for recall from the clipboard. If you "cut" another item before pasting what is currently on the clipboard, the second item will replace the current one. As a result, the first item will be lost. Therefore, it is important to "Paste" an item immediately after cutting it.

Sometimes you don't want to actually cut the material, but instead want to copy it and insert it in another part of the text. In this situation, you would use the "Copy" command from the "Edit" dropdown menu. Once again, you will need to highlight the text to be copied, and then choose "Copy" from the "Edit" dropdown menu.

The same result is achieved a bit more quickly if, after highlighting the text, you press "Ctrl" + the letter "C". After the text is copied, place the cursor at the point it is be inserted and click. "Paste" the text in the same manner described in the previous paragraph.

If you want to reverse an action recently taken (for example, you deleted some material that you meant to copy instead), you may choose "Undo" from the "Edit" dropdown menu or you may simply click on the "Undo" button on the Standard toolbar. PowerPoint remembers your last twenty actions and allows you to reverse them if necessary. However, the reversal process follows the sequence of the actions performed. In the above example, if you subsequently moved text (another action) after the accidental deletion, and then attempted to "undo" the deletion, you would first have to "undo" moving the text before you could "undo" the deletion. In this scenario, "undoing" the text movement would be necessary even though it was **not** a mistake. Therefore, it is most ideal to "Undo" an action promptly after it was taken.

Formatting Text
If you wish to emphasize certain points or just create more eye-catching messages, PowerPoint provides unique features to enhance your text's appearance.

Color
One of the most common ways to embellish your text is with color. Each bulleted point will already be displayed in the color designated on the slide master. You can change the color of the text on every slide by changing it on the Slide Master, or on individual slides by changing it in Slide View. This is accomplished by (1) highlighting the text that you wish to change, and then (2) clicking on the Font Color button on the Drawing toolbar. A box will appear displaying sixteen colors from which you may choose.

If you desire a broader selection, click on the "More Colors" box. You will be presented with a dialog box giving standard or customized color options. The standard colors option will allow you to move a pointer around a polygon containing different colored modules. As you click on each module, the new color is compared to the current text color. Clicking the "Okay" button will apply that color to the text.

Standard Colors Option Presented by Choosing "More Colors" Box

If you switch to the custom view, you will instead be allowed to modify an individual color to the intensity desired. You must first click the selection arrow somewhere within the color palette. On the right of the screen is a bar with an arrow beside it. As you move the arrow, various degrees of hue and intensity of the selected color will appear in a box at the bottom right of the screen. When you have customized the color to your satisfaction, click on the "Okay" button to apply that color to the text.

Other Ways to Alter Text

- To emphasize certain portions of your text by making it darker or **bolder,** highlight the text and then either (1) click on the "**B**" button on the formatting toolbar or (2) press "Ctrl" + the letter "B". To remove this effect, repeat the same process.

- To *italicize* text, highlight it, then (1) click on the "*I*" button on the formatting toolbar or (2) press "Ctrl" + the letter "I". To remove this effect, repeat the same process.

- To <u>underline</u> text, highlight it, then (1) click on the "<u>U</u>" button on the formatting toolbar or (2) press "Ctrl" + the letter "U". To remove this effect, repeat the same process.

- To ~~shadow~~ your text, highlight it, and click on the "S" button on the formatting toolbar. (There is no shortcut available.) To remove this effect, repeat the same process.

- To increase the size of the font, (1) highlight it, (2) then click on the larger "**A**" button on the formatting toolbar. Conversely, to decrease the font size, (1) highlight it, (2) then click on the diminutive "A" on the formatting toolbar. The font size increases and decreases at preset point size intervals.

If you want a more exact selection of font sizes, click on the arrow on the right of the Font Size button on the Formatting toolbar. A list of alternative sizes will appear. Select your preference by clicking on it. To be even more specific in determining font size, replace the current size displayed in the Font Size box by highlighting it (the cursor will change to an I-beam) and type in your own number.

To change the type of font that you are using, click on the arrow to the right of the Font Style box and browse through the choices offered. (See the example below.) Select the one you desire by clicking on it. If you would like to preview the various styles, you will need to select "Font" from the "Format" dropdown menu. As you select various font styles, the text that you have highlighted will appear in that style on the screen when you click on the preview box. Once you have decided on the appropriate style, click the "Okay" button and that style will be applied to your text.

Font Style Selections

Inserting Clip Art

If you're really intent on adding interest to your slides, try using the clip art that PowerPoint provides for its users. There are many pictures to choose from grouped in various categories ranging from animals to transportation. It's best to make the decision to use clip art when you are choosing the layout for your new slide, because at that point you can select a layout that will reserve a space for your clip art. Any text added thereafter will be positioned so that it does encroach upon the clip art. However, should you change your mind after a slide is created, you can always (1) reformat the slide's layout or (2) change the size or shape of the clipart so that it does not interfere with the text on the slide.

To best incorporate clip art into your presentation, you should be in Slide View to access the Clip Art Gallery. (It is also available in Note Pages View.) If you have chosen the layout template that has reserved a space for clip art (the one with the cartoon picture of a man), then all you need to do is to double-click on that reserved space to summon clip art. If you have not chosen this layout, then you must access Clip Art by clicking on the Clip Art button on the standard toolbar. However, if you do access clip art this way, don't be surprised where the clip art is pasted on the slide. It will be positioned right in the middle of the slide and its size will probably be much larger than you desire, especially if you plan to insert text. We'll talk about how to handle this situation later in this section. (Whichever method you use, you may be instructed to insert a clip art CD-ROM for additional pictures.)

Slide Layout with Reserved Space for Clip Art

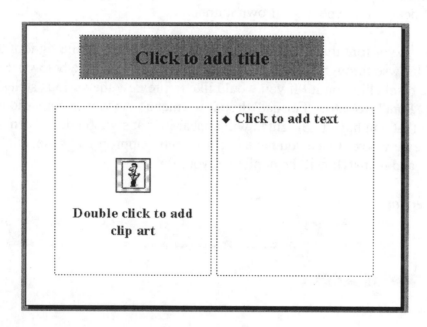

Once you've summoned the ClipArt Gallery, you may be overwhelmed with your choices. You can scroll through all the pictures (if you have enough time) by selecting All Categories from the box at the top. If you have a more specific picture in mind, however, select one of the categories where it might be found. You can then scroll through all the pictures available in that category by clicking on the up or down arrows on the scroll bar.

If you aren't quite able to determine what a picture is, select it by clicking on it (it will be outlined in black). At the bottom of the screen, you will see the title of the picture. You may also enlarge a picture by clicking on the Magnify button once the picture has been selected.

Don't be concerned if after examining the selected picture more closely, you determine it is not the picture you want. PowerPoint does not actually insert the clip art picture until you click on the Insert button on the right of the screen. Just continue to scroll through the Clip Art Gallery until you've found the picture you want, select it (the picture you selected before will then be unselected) and then click on the Insert button.

Clip Art Gallery

If you aren't sure of which category to preview in hopes of finding a certain picture, you can conduct your search by asking ClipArt to find it for you. Simply click on the Find button and type in the keyword describing the picture. Then click the "Find Now" button.

PowerPoint will either produce one or more possible pictures to fit the description or will give you a message that it could not find a match for your description. If you get the latter, it's worthwhile to try again with the description restated another way. Because PowerPoint is searching for an exact or extremely close match to the description you have given, rewording the description just slightly may increase your chances of a match.

Adjusting the Picture on the Slide
Once the clip art is pasted on your slide, chances are good that it will not be the size you need or that it will not be positioned where you would like it to be. Changing the dimensions and the position of the picture are easy tasks. The process is similar to changing the dimensions and position of text boxes, which was discussed earlier.

To re-position the picture --- Click on the picture to select it. You will see that the picture actually is enclosed in a box that allows you to treat the picture as an object. As with the text box, there will be handles on each side. Once you've clicked on the picture to reveal the four-cornered arrow, hold the clicker down and drag the picture to the desired location.

To re-size or re-shape the picture -- Click on the picture to select it. The box enclosing the picture will appear with the handles on the side. Moving the selection arrow along the edge of the box will produce a two-arrowed line. This is your signal that you can now re-size the picture. You can resize a picture in the same way you re-size a text box (see "Changing the size of a text box" on page 14.) To keep the picture from distorting, drag from the corner handle.

Background Color

Another point to remember is that PowerPoint Clip Art pictures have no background or "fill" color. Sometimes, however, background color may enhance the picture. If this is the case, you may fill the background with whatever color you want, by (1) selecting the picture, and (2) clicking on the Fill Color button (the tipped can of paint) on the Drawing toolbar.

The choices for background fill resemble the choices displayed when the Text Color button is selected. As with the selection of the Text Color button, a box containing sixteen colors for consideration appears. If you desire a broader selection of fill colors, select "More Fill Colors". Standard and customized choices then become available. When you have decided on your fill color choice, click on the "Okay" button and the new selection will replace the original background color.

Altering the Components of the Picture

You can alter many more features of the clip art picture than just its size, location and background color. With a little effort, you can change the components of the picture itself. To illustrate this process, let's assume that you have pasted onto your slide a clip art picture of a man holding a magnifying glass. The picture suits your needs with one exception: you don't want the magnifying glass. In order to eliminate it, you must separate the components of the picture with the "Ungroup" function.

Here's how this is done: First, select the picture. Then click on the "Ungroup" option from the Draw button on the Drawing toolbar. Notice that your picture has now been redefined as a group of objects comprising the picture. The Ungroup button may be clicked as many times as necessary to continue breaking down the picture into even more objects. (PowerPoint will disable the Ungroup command when the picture has been dissected as far as possible.)

After ungrouping the picture, click anywhere outside the picture to de-select the objects (they will all be selected as PowerPoint continues to ungroup). Then select the object that you wish to edit. As with any other object in PowerPoint, you may change the shape, color, or size of the object or, in our example, delete it. (See the figure on the following page.)

Step 1: Select the picture

Step 2: Click the Ungroup button

Step 3: Click on the magnifying glass

Step 4: Delete the magnifying glass

After ungrouping, you will want to regroup the objects so that PowerPoint will once again treat the objects as one picture. Otherwise, it will be difficult to move or re-size the entire picture if necessary. To do this, select all the objects in the picture again. (Hold down the shift key when selecting more than one object so that they all remain selected simultaneously). After completing the selection choose the Group option from the Draw button on the Drawing toolbar.

Hint: If the picture is the only item on the slide thus far (there is no text, for instance), it is much easier to use the "Select All" command from the "Edit" dropdown menu to regroup its components. If there are other items or text on the slide already, consider creating a blank slide just for the purpose of modifying the picture. After inserting the Clip Art onto the blank slide, you can ungroup and then alter it as desired. Once the picture is completed, use the "Select All" option from the "Edit" dropdown menu to assist in regrouping the objects. At this point you can copy it and then paste it onto the slide where it is needed.

Drawing Objects

When you are drawing in PowerPoint, you need to have the Drawing toolbar at your disposal. If it is not visible, choose the "Toolbar" command from the "View" menu and then click on "Drawing" to make it appear on your screen.

The Drawing Toolbar

While we have already discussed some of the features available with this toolbar, we'll cover some additional ones here.

Drawing Lines, Rectangles and Circles

The line button on the Drawing toolbar is depicted as a diagonal line. To draw a line on the slide, click on the line button, then place the cursor on the screen (it will be in the shape of a cross). Click where you want the line to begin and drag the cursor to where you want the line to end. When you are satisfied with the line's length, release the button.

Having a problem keeping the line straight? Hold the Shift key down while dragging the line. You can change the attributes of the line with four other buttons on the Drawing toolbar. Remember to select the line first.

- The Line Color button on the Drawing toolbar allows you to change the current line color (the default color).

- The Line Style button lets you choose the thickness of the line.

- The Dashed Lines button allows you to indicate whether you want a solid or dashed line.

- The Arrow Style button lets you place arrowheads at the beginning or end or both ends of the line.

Drawing rectangles is just as easy. Click on the rectangle button and place the cursor where you want the top corner to be positioned. Then click on the left mouse button and drag it until the rectangle has reached the desired shape. You can always modify it by selecting it, grabbing a handle and dragging it to create another shape.

If you want to create a perfect square, hold down the Shift key while dragging the mouse. If you prefer to draw from the center, rather than from the corner, hold down the Control (Ctrl) key while dragging. If you would like to draw more than one rectangle, double-click on the rectangle button. The rectangle drawing tool will then remain operative until you click on it again to turn it off. You can remove the lines defining any object you have drawn by clicking the Lines Color button on the Drawing toolbar and choosing the "No Lines" option.

In a similar fashion, circles and ovals may be drawn with the ellipse button. Drawing a circle instead of an oval requires you to hold the Shift key down while dragging the mouse.

Free Rotate
The Free Rotate button cannot be used unless you first select an object to rotate. After selecting an object, click on the button and you will see the cursor transformed into a circular arrow. Position it over a handle on the object, click, and hold it down while moving the object. The object will then be rotated around the center point (PowerPoint will indicate the number of degrees it has been rotated as you are turning it). This feature works on Clip Art pictures as well.

Filling an Object
PowerPoint automatically fills objects as they are created with a default color. If you prefer another fill color or no fill color at all, use the Fill Color button on the Drawing toolbar. You can also apply certain fill effects (shading) to the fill color by choosing the Fill Effects option revealed when the Fill Colors button is selected.

AutoShapes
Clicking on the AutoShapes button reveals eight different categories of shapes available ranging from diamonds and trapezoids to balloons and banners. If you highlight a category, the various designs associated with that category become visible. To draw a particular shape, click on it and then after positioning the cursor on the screen, click and drag until the complete shape appears. You can then resize or reposition it according to your preference.

If you'd prefer to draw your own original shape, the Freeform button lets you create whatever shape you please. Located in the Lines category under AutoShapes, the Freeform button looks like an oddly shaped polygon with some slightly curved sides. To enable this feature, click on the button, place your cursor on the screen where you want to position the first corner, click the mouse and draw. To anchor a corner, click the right or left button on the mouse. Continue drawing until you have completed the picture, then double-click.

The Draw Button on the Drawing Toolbar.
Clicking on the Draw button reveals another menu offering additional drawing features. To enable any feature, you must first select an object. Most of the options display a dialog box once selected. For example the *Rotate option* allows you to Freely Rotate, Rotate Left, Rotate Right, Flip Horizontally or Flip Vertically your selected object.

Sometimes you have objects that overlap. The *Order option* from the Draw menu allows you to Bring Forward and Send Backward the objects so that they overlap in the order you wish.

If you want to position an object that is behind another object in the front, select it and click the Bring to the Front option. Conversely, if you wish to place an object located in the front behind another object, select it, and click the Send Backward option.

If more than two objects overlap, select the object which you would like to be at the forefront and choose "Bring to the Front". Or you may select the object that you would like to be at the very back and choose "Send to the Back".

If you have several objects that you wish to align either according to their sides, tops, bottoms, or centers, select each one. (Remember to hold down the Shift key to select more than one object.) Then use the *Align option* from the Draw menu and indicate how you would like the objects arranged.

Final tips

Two final tips related to drawing with PowerPoint: If, after you have drawn an object, you would like to create an exact replica or duplicate, select the object and then press the Control key (Ctrl) + the letter "D". A second object will appear which slightly overlaps the original one. You can then move it to the location you desire on the slide. The "Duplicate" command on the "Edit" dropdown menu accomplishes the same result.

Secondly, don't forget about the Zoom button on the Standard toolbar, especially when you are drawing freeform objects. You can zoom in as close or as far out as you'd like by changing the percentage of the screen that is visible. Either click on the arrow to the right of the Zoom Control button and select a predetermined zoom percentage or replace the zoom percentage number with your own.

Charts and Graphs

The easiest way to add a chart or a graph is to choose the layout format that includes a reserved space for charts and graphs. If you create a chart or graph to be inserted on an existing slide which has no area marked for graphs or charts, the chart or graph will have to be resized.

Choosing the layout for a new slide that includes a space for a chart or graph enables you to access Microsoft Graph by merely double clicking on the reserved space. If you do not choose this option, however, you will have to access Microsoft Graph by means of the button on the Standard toolbar. If you use this option, however, the graph that will appear will be pasted right in the middle of the slide. You can easily adjust its size as you would any other object by selecting it and dragging one of the handles until it is re-sized to the desired dimensions

Microsoft Graph's Initial Screen

Microsoft
Graph
Toolbar

After you've summoned Microsoft Graph, you will be presented with a datasheet. Don't be concerned that there is already information stored there. PowerPoint uses the data that is already there to provide examples of how your data may be inputted. A column letter and a row number mark each cell's location. Fill in the data sheet as you would any spreadsheet, replacing the sample data provided.

Once Microsoft Graph is called up, you will notice that an entirely new toolbar pertaining to graph functions appears at the top of the screen. The buttons on this toolbar permit you to change number representation by columns rather than by rows, to import data from another file, to undo, cut and paste, to remove the legend, and to change the chart type.

The Microsoft Graph toolbar

If you'd like a more detailed preview of different chart types available (both in 2-D and 3-E format), choose the Chart Type button and re-format your graph however you desire. When you've completed the information on the datasheet, click anywhere outside the graph and you will be returned to your slide with the graph inserted.

If you're dissatisfied with its appearance on the slide, double-click on the graph to return to Microsoft Graph and the Graph toolbar, make any changes you'd like, and then click outside the graph to view the slide again.

IV. Creating Slides in Outline View

We've focused on creating slides in Slide View for virtually our entire discussion of PowerPoint thus far. However, as noted earlier, there are other ways to view your slides as well. Slide View is the most versatile for creating slides, but you may also develop your entire presentation or modify it by using Outline View. Outline View serves a unique function in creating and developing presentations: it forces you to focus on the text alone to the exclusion of charts, graphs, clip art, or any other enhancements to the presentation.

Outline View and Slide View work hand in hand; that is, anything you type in Outline View is simultaneously placed in Slide View format. Likewise, anything done in Slide View is simultaneously placed in Outline View format. You can switch back and forth at will when creating your presentation.

You have the option of either viewing your slides in Outline View after creating them in Slide View or initially creating your presentation in Outline view. PowerPoint will assume that you will want to create in Slide View when you begin creating the presentation.

However, when you are presented with the first slide in Slide View you can switch to Outline View by
- choosing the "Outline" command from the "View" dropdown menu or
- clicking on the Outline View button at the bottom of the screen.

Once in Outline View, a small numbered icon of a slide with the cursor positioned to its right appears. This is where you will type in the title of the slide. Also notice the Outline toolbar visible to the left of the screen.

Typing text in Outline View is similar to typing text in Slide View. In Outline View as in Slide View, PowerPoint assumes that you wish to continue a new point at the same level as the previous point. You must inform PowerPoint that you wish to type on another level if you want to add subpoints (indent to the right) or revert back to a main point (indent to the left).

As in Slide View, the text may be italicized, underlined, enlarged or reduced, or converted to bold type. Similarly, its font style may be changed. However, because the Drawing Toolbar is unavailable, if you want to change the text color you must use the Main Menu's Format command. Since the text is displayed only in black to insure that it is presented as clearly as possible, the changes to color will only be evident in the small box on the right.

A Presentation in Outline View

Outline Toolbar →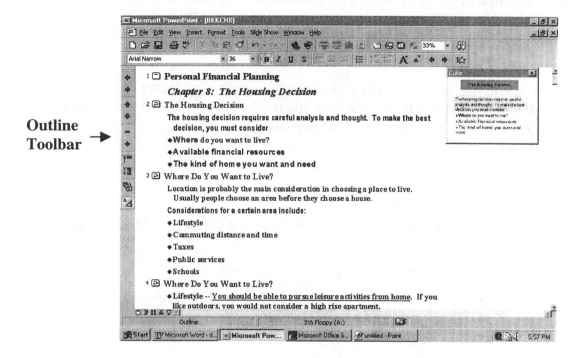

After you have typed in the title next to the slide icon and pressed "Enter", PowerPoint will display the next numbered slide icon as if you are ready to create another slide. Of course, you will probably want to type some bulleted text beneath the title, so you must tell PowerPoint that you wish to continue on the same slide with bulleted points.

There are a variety of ways to do this:

(1) Position your cursor somewhere within the line you wish to indent and click on the Demote button on the Outline toolbar. The slide icon will automatically be converted to a bullet under the previous slide's title.

(2) Place your pointer directly over the slide icon to transform the pointer into a four-arrowed pointer. Then click and drag the line to the right to automatically demote it to the next level. If you drag it still further to the right, you can demote it to any of the five levels. Each time it reaches a different level, the bullet will change shape and size and the text's appearance will be changed to reflect that level's formatted style

(3) Position your cursor somewhere within the line you wish to indent and press the Tab key. The text will be demoted to the next level. Hitting the Tab key again will demote it further until you have reached the lowest level available. Again, the formatting style will change each time you press the Tab key.

If you are distracted by the formatting and wish to eliminate it completely while developing the outline, you may remove the formatting by pressing the last button on the Outline toolbar. This, in effect, gives you the presentation stripped down to its most basic form. To restore the formatting in Outline View, click on the Formatting button again.

After typing the text on your slide and positioning it accordingly, you are ready to create a new slide. To do this, all you have to do is to reverse the demotion process described above. Your cursor will be positioned at the beginning of a new line that is at the same level as the line just typed.

To begin a new slide, your options are as follows:

1) Press the Promote button on the Outline toolbar until the slide icon appears (the highest level)

2) Place your arrow over the bullet until the four-arrowed pointer appears. Click and drag the bullet to the highest level; or

3) Place your cursor anywhere on the line and press the Shift key + the Tab key (reverses the Tab function) until the slide icon appears.

To insert a new slide between two slides that you've already created, position your cursor at the end of the last line of the slide preceding the insertion point. Click the New Slide button on the Standard toolbar and another slide icon will appear between the slides.

Viewing Slides in Outline View in Expanded or Collapsed Format

Two other tools on the Outline Toolbar allow for further options in viewing your material. If you would prefer to focus solely on one particular slide title without being distracted by the supporting information, you may "collapse" that section so that only the title of that slide is visible. Place the cursor somewhere within the slide to be collapsed and click the Collapse button on the Outline toolbar.

To restore the bulleted points on that slide, press the Expand button and once again all the information on that slide will appear. You may also achieve the same effect for the entire outline. This is accomplished by pressing the Collapse All button on the Outline toolbar. To recall all the text, press the Expand All button on the toolbar.

Collapsed Outline View

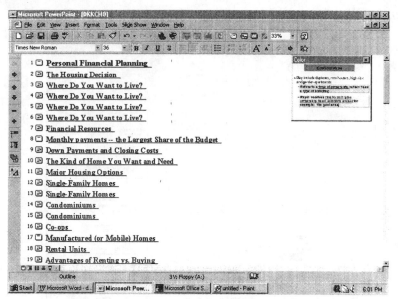

Editing Slides in Outline View

Once you've constructed your slides, you can move paragraphs (bulleted points) up or down wherever you please. Here again, the Outline Toolbar becomes useful. Place the cursor somewhere in the paragraph, and click on the Up arrow. The paragraph will jump over the one ahead of it. To move it downward, use the down arrow on the toolbar.

However, to make certain that you move the subpoints associated with a higher level point when you move that point, you should use the four-arrowed pointer. Placing the pointer over the higher level bullet and clicking it will highlight not only the higher level point, but the subpoints associated with it as well. Then you can drag the points and subpoints to a new location or use the arrows on the toolbar to reposition them.

You can also rearrange the order of the slides in the same manner. Simply use the four-arrowed pointer to highlight the slide icon and the entire slide will be selected. Then either drag the slide to another position in the outline or use the up or down arrows to reposition it.

V. Using Slide Sorter View

Slide Sorter is yet another way to obtain an overview of your entire presentation. While Outline View allows you to review your complete presentation, it is limited to text only. Slide Sorter View, on the other hand, reduces the slides (text and graphics included) and positions them in sequence. This view enables you to check the flow of the presentation and to move, add, and delete slides easily.

A Slide Presentation in Slide Sorter View

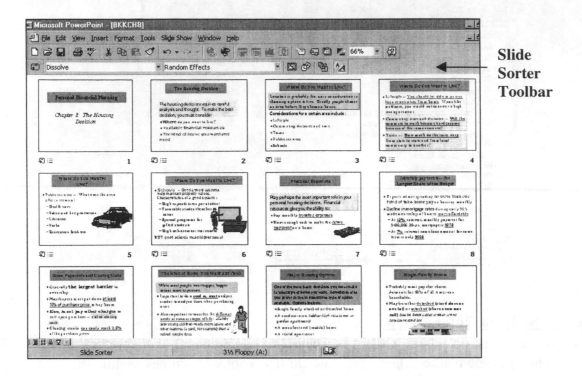

To access Slide Sorter View, click on the Slide Sorter View button on the bottom left-hand side of your screen. Once in this mode, you will see all your slides miniaturized and laid out in order. At the top of the screen, directly below the Formatting toolbar, the Slide Sorter toolbar appears. We'll discuss some of its features shortly.

Adding, Moving, and Deleting Slides
Rearranging your slides is a relatively straightforward task in Slide Sorter View. If you decide to transfer a slide from one location to another, click on that slide (a black border will appear to show that it has been selected) and while holding down the mouse button, drag it to its new position.

You can add or delete slides, also. To delete a slide, first select it. Then either
- press the backspace key;
- press the delete key; or
- choose the "Clear" command from the "Edit" dropdown menu.

To add a slide, click in between the slides where you wish to insert the new slide (a blinking cursor will appear), and press the New Slide button on the Standard toolbar. Although you have inserted a new slide, you will not be able to add any information to it without reverting to Slide View or Outline view. As noted previously, these two views are the only ones that allow for slide text creation.

The Slide Sorter Toolbar

The Slide Sorter toolbar allows you to create different effects during the slide show presentation. These effects, however, will not be visible until the slide show is actually running. (Refer to Section VII: Using the Slide Show View for more about running a slide show.) The transition effect determines how one slide transitions to the next as the presentation progresses. The animation feature determines how each bullet will appear on the screen during the presentation.

The first box on the toolbar indicates if a transition effect has been selected for a slide (in this case, the Dissolve effect is active). If no transition effect has been chosen, the words "No Transition" will appear in this box. To view the transition effects available, click on the arrow to the right of the box.

A dropdown list of transition effects will appear. As you can see from the list box, there are many different ways to introduce the slides. They may:
- dissolve in,
- checkerboard across or
- wipe from the left, right, down or up into the following slide
just to name a few.

If you'd like to keep the audience guessing as to how the next slide will transition, choose "Random Transitions" from the dropdown list. Random Transitions is a combination of all the various transition techniques. One of the techniques will be randomly applied to the slide selected. If you choose this option, even **you** will not know how the slide will appear until you run the slide show.

To incorporate the Transition effect, select a slide, and then choose a transitional technique from the transition dropdown list. Transitions occur rather quickly unless you decide otherwise. If you'd like for them to take a little longer, click on the button to the left of the Transition Effects bar to regulate the speed of the transitions.

Another option afforded by the Slide Sorter toolbar is called the animation feature, the second box displayed on the toolbar. (In the example above, "Random Effects" is the animation feature that has been selected.) If no animation feature has been selected the words "No Effect" will be displayed in the box. This option enables each bulleted point to make its own dramatic debut on the screen during a presentation. It is especially useful if:

1. you don't wish for the audience to try to absorb all the information on your slide at once or
2. you want the audience to focus solely on the point which you are discussing rather than reading ahead.

If you click on the arrow to the right of the animation features box, you will see a dropdown list of animation options. As with the transition effects, a variety of options are available. You may choose to have the bullets:

- fly from the top, bottom, left, or right
- crawl from the top, bottom, left or right or
- flash fast, medium, or slow

just to name a few. To incorporate this feature, select the slide where you wish to add the animation effect. Then choose an animation feature from the dropdown list.

Every bullet on the slide will make its appearance according to whatever feature you have chosen for that slide. However, if you would like to vary the manner in which they appear, select the "Random Effects" option. This option functions the same way as the "Random Effects" option for transition effects. PowerPoint will randomly assign an animation feature to each bullet to keep everyone (including you) in suspense.

If you want all your slides to include Animation and Transition Effects, there is no need to highlight every slide individually. The most efficient way to do this is by choosing the "Select All" command from the "Edit" menu. If you would like for most, but not all, of your slides to incorporate these effects, it's still easier to choose the "Select All" command from the "Edit" dropdown menu. You can then de-select the slides to exclude by holding down the Shift key while clicking on those slides.

Hiding Slides

One other feature of Slide Sorter view that bears mentioning is the Hide Slide function. Perhaps you have included a point in your presentation that is somewhat complex. Should the audience be unclear about the point you are making, you would like to display a slide that provides further information. However, if the audience understands the point and requires no further explanation, you would like to omit the explanatory slide. Here's where the Hide Slides function can be utilized.

If you prefer that a slide does not appear in the slide show unless it is needed, you may select that slide by clicking on it and then pressing the Hide Slide button on the Slide Sorter toolbar. If, during the presentation you need to show that slide, typing in the hidden slide number will summon it. Of course, if there is no need to reveal the slide, the slide show will continue with that slide omitted.

VI. Using Note Pages View

Unless you have an exceptionally good memory, you may require notes during your presentation. It's very uncomplicated to create slide-specific notes in PowerPoint. First, however, you must access the Note Pages View by clicking on the button on the bottom left of the screen.

PowerPoint will display each slide in a reduced format with space designated underneath the slide for you to insert notes. (You may need to scroll down on the screen to find the reserved space. You may also need to zoom in using the Zoom button on the Standard toolbar if the text is too small to read.) Once the text space is in view and you have zoomed in to a legible text size, all you have to do to begin typing is to click.

If the space reserved is too small for all your notes to fit, you can enlarge it by selecting the text box itself and then dragging one of the handles while holding down the left button on the mouse until it reaches the necessary dimensions.   You can also decrease the size of the slide on the screen in the same manner.

A Slide in Note Pages View

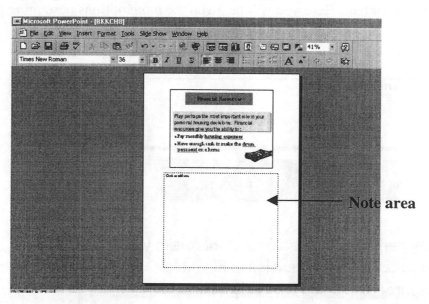

Should you find that the area provided for notes is consistently insufficient for every slide, you will need to make adjustments on the Notes Master. To summon the Note Master, hold the Shift key down while clicking on the Note Pages View button. Select the notes box and enlarge it by clicking on a handle and dragging. After this change is made on the Notes master, every slide will then contain more space for notes.

VII. Using Slide Show View

The Slide Show View is the grand finale to all your hard work. After you have finished your presentation (or if you are in the process of creating it and want to get a feel for how it will run), you can summon the Slide Show View. This is done by clicking on the Slide Show View button on the bottom left of the screen. Immediately the first slide in the presentation will expand to fill the whole screen.

If animation effects are included in the slide, each bulleted point can be introduced by
    (1) hitting the Enter key;
    (2) clicking the left button on the mouse or
    (3) pressing the Space Bar.

Transitioning to the next slide is also accomplished by any of the same three methods just described if the last bulleted point on the current slide has been revealed. Clicking on the right mouse button during the Slide Show enables you to move more randomly through the presentation rather than sequentially by engaging the Slide Navigator. To exit the Slide Show View before the presentation's completion, press the Escape key.

If you'd like to be more detailed in how the Slide Show should unfold, select "Slide Show" from the menu bar. Here you will be given the more options pertaining to the show's viewing

A Slide in Slide Show View

Financial Resources

Play perhaps the most important role in your personal housing decisions. Financial resources give you the ability to:

- ◆ Pay monthly <u>housing expenses</u>
- ◆ Have enough cash to make the <u>down payment</u> on a home

VIII. Printing

PowerPoint enables you to print anything that you've created in different formats. To invoke the Printing function you may: (1) hold the Control (Ctrl) key down while pressing the letter "P" or (2) choose the "Print" command from the "File" dropdown menu. A Print dialog box appears asking you what you want to print.

The first section of the dialog box identifies your printer. The next section asks you to indicate the range of the presentation you would like to print. You can click in the "All" box if you want to print the entire presentation, or you can limit the printing to the current page or a range of pages. To specify a certain range to be printed, click on "Slides" and then type in the page numbers.

The next section in the dialog box asks what you want to print. Unless you are planning to use your slides for overheads, you probably won't need to print them. However, if you do, you may print the slides without animation effects. You can also print the outline or handouts for the audience (with two, three, or six slides on each page). If you've typed notes in Note Pages View, you will most certainly choose the Notes Pages option. To select any option, highlight it, and then click the "Okay" button.

The Print Dialog Box

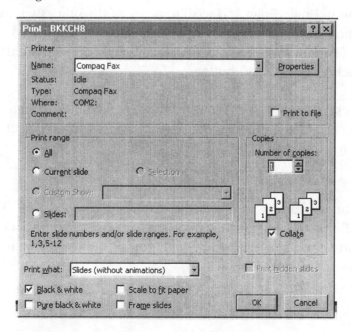

IX. Saving and Exiting PowerPoint

Before exiting PowerPoint, first save your work and then close the file (or files) that is currently open. To save your work, either choose "Save" from the "File" dropdown menu or press the Control key ("Ctrl") + the letter "S".

Close your file by either choosing the "Close" command from the "File" dropdown menu or clicking on the box containing the "X" on the menu bar. If you have forgotten to save your work before attempting to close the file, PowerPoint will remind you with a message asking if you want to save the file.

If you choose the "Yes" button, your work will automatically be saved. Exiting the PowerPoint program is accomplished by clicking on the box with the "X" on the program title bar or by choosing "Exit" from the "File" dropdown menu.

X. Modifying an Existing Presentation

There are two ways to open an existing presentation to modify it, depending on whether PowerPoint is up and running or not. If you have just opened PowerPoint, you will be presented with options pertaining to creating a new presentation (AutoContent Wizard, Template, Blank Presentation) or of Opening an Existing Presentation. Select the last option ("Open an Existing Presentation") and click "Okay". A list of files will appear. As you highlight each file, you can view the first slide of that file in the preview box. Once you've highlighted the file you want, click on the "Open" button and the file will appear.

If you are already working in PowerPoint and wish to access a file other than the one you have been working on, choose "Open" from the "File" dropdown menu. This command will cause the same list of files described above to appear. You can then highlight the one that you need and click on the "Okay" button.

Modifying an existing presentation is no different from working on an original file. You may make any text, color, or graphic changes you please. Be sure to save your work before closing the file to retain the changes.

XI. In Summary

This concludes the brief tutorial describing the basic features of PowerPoint. The only way to fully appreciate all that the program has to offer is by experimenting with it yourself. Once you become familiar with PowerPoint, you'll find it to be an invaluable tool for developing show-stopping presentations.